The **LITTLE** Book
— OF —

BIG
F**K UPs

220 of HISTORY'S MOST-
**REGRETTABLE
MOMENTS**

KEN LYTLE & KATIE CORCORAN LYTLE, MA
Foreword by BOB CARNEY, *founder and owner of* STUMP! TRIVIA

Aadamsmedia
AVON, MASSACHUSETTS

Published by
Adams Media, a division of F+W Media, Inc.
57 Littlefield Street, Avon, MA 02322. U.S.A.
www.adamsmedia.com

ISBN 10: 1-4405-1252-3
ISBN 13: 978-1-4405-1252-0
eISBN 10: 1-4405-2500-5
eISBN 13: 978-1-4405-2500-1

Printed in the United States of America.

10 9 8 7 6 5 4 3 2 1

Library of Congress Cataloging-in-Publication Data
is available from the publisher.

This publication is designed to provide accurate and authoritative information with
regard to the subject matter covered. It is sold with the understanding that the
publisher is not engaged in rendering legal, accounting, or other professional advice.
If legal advice or other expert assistance is required, the services of a competent
professional person should be sought.
—From a *Declaration of Principles* jointly adopted by a Committee of the American
Bar Association and a Committee of Publishers and Associations

This book is available at quantity discounts for bulk purchases.
For information, please call 1-800-289-0963.

DEDICATION

———◆———

To our parents: Joy, Larry, Gary, and Ellen for teaching us how to get through all the little disasters that life has thrown at us—and for loving us even when we f*#k up.

ACKNOWLEDGMENTS

While we were writing this book, we were going through a little disaster of our own: a complete renovation of the top floor of our home. We'd like to thank everyone who helped us out so we'd have the time to write about other people's disasters—which made us feel a little better about our own.

So without further ado, we'd like to thank our parents above all for always believing in us (and being good at manual labor), Patti "The Cupcake" Corcoran for doing our dishes and always making us laugh, Rachael Lytle for keeping us in good spirits throughout the process, and to our friends for telling us how awesome we are when we thought we were in over our heads.

We'd also like to thank everyone who believed in and worked on our book, especially Karen Cooper, Jon Ackerman, Paula Munier, Beth Gissinger-Rivera, Wendy Simard, Frank Rivera, Meredith O'Hayre, Casey Ebert, Jeff Litton, Ashley Vierra, and Sheila Elmosleh.

Thanks for helping us make our little book a big success.

Katie and Ken

CONTENTS

1930 Welcome to the Dirty Thirties

1931 Tax Fraud? Really?

1933 Strike a Pose

1934 Don't Touch That!

1937 The Big Bang Theory

1937 Happy Holidays!

1938 Chiang Kai-shek's Spineless Decision

1939 Ye Olde Line of Defense

1939 The Throws of the *Thetis*

1940 A Thrill Ride Over Puget Sound

1941 A Date Which Lives in Infamy

1942 How Much? For What? Pfffft!

1944 The Day the Clowns Cried

1944 Handle with Care

1944 Hawaii Uh-Oh

1945 Whoa . . . When Did THAT Get There?

1945 S*#t Happens

1945 The USS *Wherethehellisit*

1948 When Conventional Wisdom Doesn't Hold True

1949 Aw Nuts!

1954 Elvis Has Left the Building

1955 Go, Speedracer, Go!

1956 Full Steam Ahead!

1959 The Ultimate Lemon

1959 The Great Leap Backward

1960 Patience Is a Virtue

1961 Camelot Versus Castro

1962 Houston, We Have a Typo

1962 While My Guitar Gently Weeps

1963 An Italian Disastro

1963 You Don't Always Get What You Pay For

1964 The Happiest Place on Earth?

1967 What's This Schlitz in My Beer?

1967 Can't See the *Forrestal* Through the Flames

1968 Do Not Adjust Your TV Sets . . .

1972 Is It Over Yet?

1972 Tricky Dick

1973 May the Force Be With You, Mr. Lucas

1974 Ten-Cent Beer Night— No, Really

1974 Flixborough's Chemical Romance

1992 Dan Quayle: Spelling Chump

1993 Hurry Up and Finish, Even if It's Wrong!

1993 UNC Has It Handed to Them . . . Again

1995 Not Guilty? Come Again?

1995 It Was Divine

1995 You Can't Beat the Original

1995 What Goes Up, Must Come Down

1998 The St. Cloud Gas Explosion

1998 The Yaoundé Train Explosion

1998 Love That Dirty Water

1998 Who Lost the Death Pool?

1999 It's a Bird . . . It's a Dinosaur . . . It's an Archaeoraptor!

1998 The Great Zippergate

1999 Excite's Exciting Opportunity . . . Thrown Away

1999 The Thrill of Victory and the Agony of Defeat

2000 Y2K: The End of the World?

2001 Enron's Charmed Life

2002 I Could Swear They Were Here a Second Ago!

2002 Keep the Coffee Coming

2003 A Foul Play on a Foul Ball

2003 No Move Is a Bad Move

2003 Grizzly Man's Last Voyage

2003 Don't Hold Your Breath!

2004 The Dean Scream

2004 Down in Front, Larry!

2004 Nipplegate

2005 Six of One, a Half Dozen of the Other

2006 What's a Little Birdshot Between Friends

2006 A Million Little Mistakes

2007 When You Gotta Go, You Gotta Go

2007 Truss No One

2008 From Moment of Truth to Moment of Fiction

2009 Egyptian Train Crash

2009 Good Stuff! Cheap!

2009 The Red-Handed Balloon

2010 F*#k Up at the Redneck Riviera

2010 Someone Give the Owner an Owner's Manual

2010 The Imperfect Game

2010 The Train to Nowhere

FOREWORD

My mother got me interested in trivia when I was in high school, right around the same time Trivial Pursuit debuted their classic game. Just like a lot of people reading this now, we would play that game, again and again, until we had every question memorized. My mother is why I became a history major in college, and she is the sole reason why I started Stump! Trivia Quiz twelve years ago. Unfortunately, she passed away five months after I started my first pub trivia event. She would love this book.

Since starting Stump! Trivia, I've met a lot of people that are very excited (almost crazy!) about trivia—Ken and Katie are two of those people. They always loved coming out to play pub quizzes, and elaborating with the host on the things that they know . . . until Ken started running his own Stump! Trivia events. After that happened, trivia kind of took over their lives. So when they asked me to me to write a foreword for a book they were writing I was a little intrigued. I know how passionate they are about trivia, and a book about the biggest F ups of all time? *That* could be interesting. Actually for the most part, if something has to do with trivia, you can count me in, and after reading the book, I'm glad I said yes.

Sometimes people do things that are just so stupid that a simple Q and A doesn't give you enough information. You walk away asking yourself, *How on earth could* that *happen?* And *that* is why this book is so great. This book gives you detailed reasons why these 220 blunders occurred, in most cases thanks to some idiot who made a wrong decision and will forever live in infamy (especially now that this book has been written). The authors have combined bizarre and unbelievable facts and factiods with a great sense of humor and a generous shot of sarcasm (and maybe even a splash of mockery every now and then).

So get ready to laugh and mock with the best of them. Be sure to study up on these 220 blunders, because if they haven't been included in a Stump! Trivia question yet, they soon will be at an event near you.

Bob Carney, founder and owner of Stump! Trivia

www.stumptrivia.com

INTRODUCTION

The Trojan Horse. The Hindenburg. The Balloon Boy fiasco. What a cluster of calamities. One day you're accepting a gift from a penitent Greek, the next you wake up with a spear in your face wondering what went wrong. One second you're taking a Jerseylicious trip to the Shore on a state-of-the-art airship, the next you're plunging to the ground in a hot-as-hell fireball because someone thought flammable paint was a good idea. What it all boils down to is this: Nobody's perfect. At one point or another, you've cut someone off in traffic, forgot your wedding anniversary, or missed a big meeting because you were busy updating your Facebook status. We all mess up. *C'est la vie.* Right?

Wrong. Let's just call a spade a spade and agree that when people f*#k up on a large, game-changing scale, we should mock them. Relentlessly. For centuries on end. Think about it: There are morons out there who have scuttled ships, downed aircraft, and sunk presidential campaigns with simple, mindless acts of sheer stupidity. We shouldn't have to give these half-wits a hug and tell them that they'll do better next time!

But let's get serious for a second. While you make fun of these disaster-causing dimwits, keep in mind the old saying that history repeats itself. And you don't want any of these mishaps coming back to rear their ugly heads a second time around. This is why *The Little Book of Big F*#k Ups* takes you on a death-defying walk from the beginning of time through the present to take a look at history's most screwed-up scenarios. Here you'll hear voices from the past in the form of historical quotes and learn lessons that will leave you riveted to the spot, unable to look away, such as:

- Never trust a dyslexic stockbroker
- Don't search for a gas leak while holding a lit blowtorch
- Sometimes autopilot isn't the best idea
- An improperly flushed toilet can sink more than your dinner plans

And . . .

- Arsenic and sugar look a lot alike. So if you have both lying around (and who doesn't), it might be a good idea to pull out that old label maker.

Sounds fun, right?

So, grab your gas masks, hoard your canned goods, and be glad you weren't involved in any of the major mistakes you're about to shake your head at. Let the mockery begin!

ORIGINAL SIN

And when the woman saw that the tree was good for food, and that it was a delight to the eyes, and that the tree was to be desired to make one wise, she took of the fruit thereof, and did eat; and she gave also unto her husband with her, and he did eat.

—Genesis 3:6

Whether you think the Bible is a big book of mythology or a Dear Diary entry written exclusively by the big guy upstairs, you have to admit that the original f*#k up was a doozy.

Adam and Eve were living the good life in the nudist colony that was the Garden of Eden. They didn't have to go to work. They lived in an idyllic climate. God delivered takeout to them a few times a day—and all he asked was that they leave his damn produce alone. They were pretty much good to go . . . until Eve decided she wanted to go apple picking. Eve didn't have the option of calling her sister or childhood friends to partake so she prodded her man (hell, at that point, the only man), Adam, who reluctantly agreed to go along.

And so Eve decided she wanted the one thing she wasn't supposed to have: an apple from the Tree of Knowledge. She gave in to temptation, then convinced Adam to join in her misbehavior. God was pissed, and kicked Adam and Eve out of his house and punished mankind by making us all grow our own food and experience natural childbirth. Nicely done, first family. F*#kers!

1184 B.C.

Beware of Greeks Bearing Gifts

> This hollow fabric either must inclose,
> Within its blind recess, our secret foes; . . .
> Somewhat is sure design'd, by fraud or force:
> Trust not their presents, nor admit the horse.

—Laocoon in Virgil's *Aeneid*

According to legend, by 1184 B.C. the Trojans and the Greeks had been warring for ten long years over the beautiful Helen of Troy. (Apparently the fact that she had left Greece—and her husband—of her own free will didn't make a lick of difference to those fighting for her return.) Tired of fighting, the Greeks decided to take things into their own hands and built a huge horse that they hoped the Trojans would take as an "okay, you win" present, which is exactly what they did. The Trojans pulled the horse into their beleaguered city and celebrated their "victory." However, once night fell the sneaky Greeks who had hidden inside the massive horse (surprise!) spilled out onto the streets of Troy and pretty much killed anyone who had been stupid enough to believe that they would just give up and leave.

Let's break this down: A huge wooden horse that was large enough to contain roughly forty Greeks, the belief that the Greeks would just give up after fighting for Helen for ten long years, and a warning from a respected Trojan priest who pretty clearly laid out the Greeks' plan. Sounds like the Trojans got just what they deserved.

A HORSE OF A F*#KED-UP COLOR

Today, a Trojan horse is a malware program that software giant Cisco describes as "a harmful piece of software that looks legitimate. Users are typically tricked into loading and executing it on their systems."

XERXES: GREEK FOR "POMPOUS ASS"

I am Xerxes, great king, king of kings, the king of all countries which speak all kinds of languages, the king of the entire big far-reaching earth.

—Xerxes himself

Persian king Xerxes was moving right along in his rampage through Greece. His main strength was the large quantity of naval vessels that he used in his conquests, which often outnumbered all of what Greece had in their fleet. Xerxes needed his navy to help supply his large army, and this was a facet of his charge that the Greeks would attempt to exploit in their efforts to put a stop to Xerxes's run. Due to the combined actions of his large naval fleet and accompanying army, Xerxes scored relatively easy victories as he advanced along the coast. Not surprisingly the king developed a god complex where he felt like he could not be stopped, but his cockiness soon got in the way of his battle acumen and stopped him dead in his tracks.

While preparing to mount an attack on the Peloponnesian peninsula, Xerxes was accosted by an escaped Greek slave who informed him that the Greek fleet was fighting amongst each other and would soon side with Xerxes in an effort to prevent war. This didn't seem right, did it? Would the self-proclaimed "king of kings" really listen to an escaped slave? Why yes, he would. Xerxes turned his fleet around and headed out of the Peloponnesian peninsula . . . right into the waiting Greek fleet. Hook, line, and sinker. Xerxes's ships, which were much larger and less mobile than the Greek ships, couldn't maneuver and were essentially trapped in the peninsula. One by one his ships—and all of the men on them—went down. With the fleet gone, Xerxes couldn't support his massive army and was left to retreat out of Greece with what he had left.

Xerxes thought he had it all figured out, but one pesky peon had his day in the sun and ensured Greece of its independence.

413 B.C.

A Dark Day in Syracuse

And when all were in readiness, and none of the enemy had observed
them, not expecting such a thing, the moon was eclipsed in the night, to
the great fright of Nicias and others, who, for want of experience, or out
of superstition, felt alarm at such appearances.

—Plutarch

The Second Battle of Syracuse was a stunning defeat for the Athenians
during the Peloponnesian War. They had already lost a lot of men when the
Syracusans pretended to retreat and, instead, attacked the Athenians just as
they sat down for some celebratory baklava. In addition, there was a threat
of a Spartan invasion in the Greek region of Attica that was probably more
important to win. Mulling this over, the Athenian commander Nicias decided
to retreat with his army—if not his pride—intact. He was all ready to sneak
out of Syracuse when disaster struck in the form of . . . a lunar eclipse.

Now, we all know how scary a shadow can be, so it makes total sense that
Nicias decided to delay his army's retreat by twenty-seven days. The end result?
The Syracusans' block of the Athenians' escape route, the execution of Nicias,
the enslavement of his army, and, eventually, the overthrow of the democratic
Athenian government. And all because Nicias was afraid of a shadow.

NOTHING LIKE NATURE (AND A COUPLE VIRGINS) TO SAVE THE DAY

The most famous solar eclipse happened in 585 B.C. The Lydians and
the Persians were all lined up to battle it out when the sun went dark.
Instead of fighting, a peace treaty was drawn up and two marriages
took place to seal the deal. Who knows how many battles could have
been avoided just by turning off the lights.

The Socratic Suicide

Squeezing a foot hard, [the attendant] asked him if he felt anything.
Socrates said that he did not. He did the same to his calves and, going
higher, showed us that he was becoming cold and stiff. Then he felt him a
last time and said that when the poison reached the heart he would be gone.

—Plato, Socrates's student

Socrates had quite the resume: philosopher, teacher of Aristotle and Plato, and inventor of the Socratic Method. You'd think that such a man would be respected, but over the years Socrates had done a few things that really pissed off the democratic government in Greece.

In fact, Athens brought Socrates to court on charges of impiety, a refusal to believe in the Greek gods (which makes sense; who wouldn't believe in gods who threw thunderbolts and were obsessed with sleeping with mortal women?), and of corrupting the youth of the city by sharing his ideas with them. He was found guilty, and the jury proposed the death penalty as punishment (seems a bit harsh, no?). Then they asked Socrates what he thought his punishment should be. Instead of taking things seriously, Socrates suggested that Athens reward him for educating her citizens. Let's just say that the Athenian government didn't appreciate Socrates's sense of humor.

The philosopher was forced to commit suicide by drinking hemlock, a poison that paralyzes the central nervous system and eventually stops the heart, when all he had to do was suggest a realistic punishment. Maybe he wasn't the brightest priest at the Parthenon. See where sarcasm gets you?

WIELD YOUR SCEPTER WISELY

A Celt stroked the beard of one of them, Marcus Papirius, which he wore long as they all did then, at which point the Roman struck him over the head with his ivory mace, and, provoking his anger, was the first to be slain. After that, the rest were massacred where they sat.

—Livy, Roman historian

By the time the Gauls made it into Rome in 390 B.C., they had been besieging the city for seven months. Rome was a tough nut to crack, and when they finally breached the city walls, what they found was a ghost town. Almost every single Roman remaining had retreated to the Citadel, which was easier to defend. However, the Roman senators decided they were so freakin' important that their presence distracted the soldiers protecting the city and were sitting outside the Citadel when the Gauls approached—just waiting to be collateral damage. Next thing you know, one of the senators hit a Gaul over the head with his scepter and all hell broke loose. All the senators were killed and the city was set on fire.

The Gauls never did break into the Citadel; the Romans eventually paid them 1,000 pounds of gold to go away. If it weren't for the arrogance of the senators, chances are that the Gauls would have left the city in better shape and some government officials would have been left alive to take charge. Senators, the next time the Gauls come a knocking, leave your egos at the Citadel door!

▬ MOTHER GOOSE HAS GOT YOUR BACK ▬

One of the Gauls' best attempts to get into Rome was actually thwarted when the sacred geese of the Temple of Juno started honking, alerting the Roman soldiers of the attack. Silly geese!

---

217 B.C.

HMM . . . WHY IS THAT LAKE RED?

Though every other person in the council advised safe rather than showy measures, urging that he should wait for his colleague, in order that joining their armies, they might carry on the war with united courage and counsels . . . Flaminius, in a fury . . . gave out the signal for marching for battle.

—Livy, Roman historian

Usually, the rule is that you don't f*#k with Rome, but in the Second Punic War, the rule was more likely don't f*#k with Hannibal, the leader of the Carthaginians. Hannibal was raised to hate Rome and took warfare against them to a whole new level. In 217 B.C., Hannibal spent his time trying to taunt Roman consul Flaminius into fighting him. At first Flaminius wouldn't budge, but then Hannibal marched around Flaminius, severing the consul's route to Rome (which is, after all, where all roads lead). Flaminius had had enough and, against the advice of his advisors who suggested he wait for reinforcements, headed out after Hannibal in a rage.

Unfortunately for the Romans, Hannibal had a feeling Flaminius would come after him and was lying in wait. The consul led his army right into Hannibal's trap, and Flaminius and 15,000 Roman soldiers were taken out in roughly four hours. Local legends say that the lake was red with blood for days after the Battle of Lake Trasimene. A few days later, Hannibal also defeated the reinforcements that Flaminius should have waited for. See what happens when people can't play nice?

A TACTICAL ERROR

In an ironic twist, Rome actually stole many of Hannibal's techniques and used them to strengthen their empire. Bet Hannibal was rolling in his grave.

48 B.C.

LIBRICIDE, ROMAN STYLE

When the enemy endeavored to cut off his communication by sea, he was forced to divert that danger by setting fire to his own ships, which, after burning the docks, thence spread on and destroyed the great library.

—Plutarch

World domination and book burning typically go hand in hand. The Spanish bishop of Yucatan burned all but three of the sacred texts of the ancient Mayan civilization. Adolf Hitler and the Nazis burned books by scientists, humanists, and Jewish authors. And Julius Caesar burned the largest collection of knowledge in the world at the time: the Royal Library of Alexandria in Egypt. Why would Julius Caesar, orator and lover of knowledge, burn down the first international library, an institution that was home to original scrolls by philosophers and playwrights such as Aeschylus, Sophocles, and Euripides? According to Greek historian Plutarch, it was just a big ol' f*#k up.

Turns out that Caesar was trying to take over the city when, in a strategic move, he set fire to his own fleet—and subsequently took out more than he bargained for. The lesson here? Render to Caesar anything that Caesar wants, or he'll burn your house—and ship . . . and docks . . . and centuries worth of culture—to the ground.

NOTHING LIKE SOUTHERN HOSPITALITY

In 1966, John Lennon made the mistake of claiming that the Beatles were "more popular than Jesus." People throughout the South angrily responded by setting their Beatles records on fire. The Ku Klux Klan got involved and actually nailed a Beatles record to a cross before lighting the match. Point well taken.

---

44 B.C.

ET TU, BRUTE?

Are you a man to pay attention to a woman's dreams and the idle gossip of stupid men . . . listen to me, cast aside the forebodings of all these people, and come.

—Marcus Brutus, Roman senator (as reported by Nicolaus of Damascus)

If you've sat through a college Shakespeare course, chances are you've heard the words, "Et tu, Brute?" ("And you, Brutus?")—the last words out of the mouth of Julius Caesar before he succumbed to the stab wounds inflicted by his fellow senators. The fact that his BFF Marcus Brutus was wielding one of the knives only added insult to injury.

Caesar seemed pretty shocked by the whole situation, which is surprising to anyone with access to a history book since it seems that he was fairly well warned of what was going to happen. Pretty much everyone Caesar knew tried to convince him not to go to the Senate that day. His friends had all heard rumors that something bad was going to go down. His doctors told him to take a sick day. And his wife had a vision the night before that foretold Caesar's death.

But did he listen? Nope. He let Brutus convince him he would be seen as a complete wuss if he stayed home. So, throwing caution to the wind, off he went to his death. But at least he died with his pride intact . . .

Moron.

NO ONE EVER SAID THE SECRET SERVICE WAS KID FRIENDLY

In 1963, the *Toronto Star* reported that a little boy tried to talk to JFK just minutes before he was gunned down. Supposedly, the boy frantically chased after the car shouting, "Slow down. For God's sake, slow down!" The boy was thrown to the ground by a Secret Service agent and was never heard from again.

---

27 B.C.

When It All Comes Crashing Down

One Atilius, of the freedman class, having undertaken to build an amphitheatre at Fidena for the exhibition of a show of gladiators, failed to lay a solid foundation to frame the wooden superstructure with beams of sufficient strength; for he had neither an abundance of wealth, nor zeal for public popularity, but he had simply sought the work for sordid gain.

—Tacitus, *The Annals*

Dealing with contractors sucks. Everything is always over budget. Nothing's ever finished on time. The stuff you want done isn't done right. It's frustrating, but take comfort in the fact that this type of tomfoolery has been going on for centuries.

In 27 B.C., Atilius set to work building the Fidenae amphitheater. Unfortunately, he didn't take the time to make sure the foundation was structured properly. But no one seemed to care; they just wanted to watch gladiators kill each other.

Psyched that their favorite shows were back on after their former emperor Tiberius had outlawed the gladiator spectacles, close to 50,000 people swarmed to the Fidenae amphitheater to watch the games. The weight of all those bloodthirsty people shifted the foundation and buckled the stadium. Close to 20,000 died, lazy Atilius was run out of town, and a town building inspector was hired. Looks like the Fidenae townsfolk should have checked Atilius's references before forking over all of their hard earned *solidus*.

A.D. 61

Don't F*#k with Rome

Ignore the racket made by these savages . . . They are not soldiers—they're not even properly equipped. We've beaten them before and when they see our weapons and feel our spirit, they'll crack.

—Suetonius, Roman commander (as reported by Tacitus, Roman historian)

In A.D. 61, Britain (along with everywhere else) was occupied by Rome. The Brits weren't thrilled with this to begin with, but when the Romans started exerting their force, the Brits decided they had had enough.

Boudicca, the widow of a tribal British king whose lands had been confiscated by Rome, took matters into her own hands at the Battle of Watling Street. She put together a huge army of rebel soldiers (the majority untrained) and declared war. On paper it looked like a good idea. The Roman commander, Suetonius, had only 10,000 troops at his disposal, and the rebels were fighting on home soil.

The mistake? Forgetting all the military training and experience the Roman soldiers had after years of kicking ass. As the Britons advanced, they were totally undone by the Romans' superior armor, weapons, and training. Close to 80,000 Britons lost their lives that day, compared to only 400 Romans. The lesson? Don't f*#k with Rome, unless you're 100 percent sure you're going to win.

AT LEAST THEY HAVE THE FRENCH KISS

In 1415, the Britons redeemed themselves by winning the Battle of Agincourt. This time around, the Britons held the upper hand with superior weapons and strategy; 6,000 soldiers led by Henry VI defeated a French force of more than 30,000. Bad day to be French.

FOR HE'S (NOT) A JOLLY GOOD FELLOW

At last, I can begin to live like a human being.

—Nero, upon completion of his Roman palace

It's been said that Rome wasn't built in a day—and apparently it doesn't take much longer than that to burn it down. With most of Rome consisting of wooden buildings, it took just six days for a fire to torch the city.

It is widely believed that Nero, emperor at the time, intentionally set Rome on fire and gleefully watched it burn to the ground. Seeing his destruction firsthand, Nero said that he was "ambitious to found a new city to be called after himself." Nero's ego was growing, and it wasn't over yet. His new palace—which he naturally called the Golden House of Nero—contained a humongous statue right at the entrance. Who was the statue a likeness of? Why, it was Nero! Perhaps his swollen head made up a majority of the 120 feet in height.

On the bright side (kind of), Nero did make a (lame) effort to prove to the citizens that he had a heart. He funded a relief effort and opened his palaces to house the homeless and gave them food to prevent starvation. He did burn down their houses and all of their possessions in them, so it's only fair that he find some place for them to live while he builds the city back up again, right? What a swell guy!

NOTHING LIKE TAKING THE EASY WAY OUT

Nero's greed caught up with him in 68 when a mass rebellion resulted from his strict tax policies. Rather than being beaten to death by the angry mob, he committed suicide instead. Looks like he was crazy *and* brave.

140

"LOOK AT ME! LOOK AT ME!"

He was so high-minded and generous that, after enlarging and embellishing the Circus, which had crumbled away in places, he merely inscribed on it a statement that he had made it adequate for the Roman people.

—Dio, Roman historian

Ah, the circus. Clowns. Acrobats. Dogs dressed up in outfits made to do stupid tricks. Although that sounds lovely, that's not exactly what the Circus Maximus in Rome was used for back in the day. Back then, Romans went to the Circus to see gladiators, chariot racing, wild animal hunts, and, last but not least, politicians and emperors. Gotta grab some fried dough for all that fun!

The Circus Maximus was destroyed by fire in 31 and 64. Each time it was rebuilt, the current ruler added his stamp to the structure. In 103, Emperor Trajan took over and went a little nuts. He rebuilt the Circus in marble, reworked the box seats to make it look like he were sitting in a temple, and increased the viewing space so the Circus could hold close to 250,000 people seated—and close to an additional 250,000 for standing-room only. Why did he do all this? Arrogance. He wanted more people to be able to see him at the Circus as the head of Rome. Trajan (who died in A.D. 117) got what he wanted, but he added so much weight with his vain remodel that the structure just couldn't stand the test of time. It collapsed in 140, killing more than 1,000 people. The Circus Maximus stadium collapse is still the most deadly sports disaster today. Talk about vanity being a deadly sin!

SEE, IT IS DANGEROUS

The famous chariot race in *Ben-Hur* (1959) was filmed in a replica of the Circus Maximus. Contrary to popular belief, no one died during the filming. However, in an earlier version of the film, released in 1926, a stuntman did die when the wheel of his chariot fell off.

⇒◦⇐

HOLD YOUR FIRE!

[The Goths were] a splendid recruiting ground for my army.
—Valens, Roman emperor at the time of the attack

It only takes one person to ruin the fun for everybody else. In the case of a single Roman soldier, his stupidity led to centuries of doom for his country.

The tension between the Goths (the barbarian warriors, not the dark, emo teenage crowd) and Romans was so thick you could cut it with a sword. Having entered Rome with permission due to discord in eastern Europe (where they were forced out by the Huns), the Goths were disruptive to the point that the Romans decided to kick the Goths out and restore peace. Leaving a war-torn area only to start another one in an intended safe haven does not make a good first impression.

So rather than mount an attack against each other, the Romans and Goths were in the process of working out a peaceful agreement that would allow them to coexist. Both sides were wary, but they were making progress. Then, without warning or reason, one Roman soldier fired a single arrow in the direction of the Goths. So much for peace. The Goths fired back and the battle was on. The Goth army, which had more manpower and more experienced fighters, overtook the weaker Romans and finally found their safe haven from the Huns after six years of war. And Rome found themselves screwed . . . thanks to one stinkin' arrow.

> **WAR IS OVER (BUT NOT FOR LONG)**
>
> The Goths got their peace but lost it in less than a century as constant invasions from other barbarian groups led to the sharing of the empire. These guys just can't get it right, can they?

453

——◆——

THAT BLOODTHIRSTY HUN

Who can rate this as death, when none believes it calls for vengeance?
—Jordanes, Roman historian

Attila the Hun: Fearsome warrior. Leader of the Huns. Dedicated enemy of the Roman empire. All-around tough guy. Quite fitting that he suffered a bloody death then, right? Well, not exactly . . . .

Attila got married in 453 to a lovely young lady named Illdico (not his first wife by any means; the Hun was a stud). Attila, not being known for his manners, got insanely drunk at the wedding. Sounds fun, but it didn't end up being his perfect day. Attila suffered from frequent nosebleeds and had one on his wedding night. On a normal day, this wouldn't be a problem. He'd pinch his nose, stuff some Kleenex up there, and get to the dirty task of killing Romans. However, on his wedding night he was passed out drunk. During the night the bloodthirsty bridegroom met his end, not at the tip of a sword, but by choking to death on the blood from his own nosebleed. What a nerdy way for a badass to die.

WHAT A WAY TO GO!

According to the U.S. Centers for Disease Control and Prevention, nosebleeds contribute to approximately four deaths in the United States per year. Bloody horrible!

985

LACK OF GREENLAND

Men will desire much the more to go there if the land has a good name.

—Erik the Red

Erik the Red wasn't exactly the brightest crayon in the box, as evidenced by his foray into the place he would call Greenland. A nomad who fled his home country of Norway in 982, he ventured upon a land blanketed in ice with a few green fields to the west of Norway. After exploring this new territory for a few years, while also discovering the harsh climate and lack of trees, he decided to call this place his own. In a move of marketing genius, Erik the Red called this barren place Greenland in an effort to attract settlers—and it worked.

On a journey to Iceland (which is actually green), he convinced a group to go back with him and set up camp. On a land covered in ice, farming was out of the question so the settlers resorted to trading to survive. Erik forged west into North America to stir up some partners but died before any successful trade routes could be established. Now his "faithful" followers were stuck on a virtual sheet of ice, foraging for wood for housing and living off of what they could catch in the ocean. No wood for housing meant no wood for ships, so they were stuck in Greenland. At least it sounds pretty.

NOTHING HAS CHANGED

The estimated 2010 population of Greenland was 56,452, which comes out to .069 people per square mile (compared to 83 per square mile for the United States). Still no green land there.

999

Y1K

Some were certain that the Second Coming of Christ would fall on the last day of the last year, 999, at the very stroke of midnight.

—Richard Erdoes, *A.D. 1,000: Living on the Brink of Apocalypse*

You remember Y2K, right? Would the world end? Would the lights go out? Would computers rise up and decide it was kill time? Well, back in 999 people felt exactly the same way—only without the added excitement of possible death by computer.

Back then, religious folks figured that 1,000 years after the birth of Christ was the perfect time for him to come back, kick ass, and take names, but they weren't sure exactly when everything would go down. As a result, people spent the entirety of 999 acting like they were going to die tomorrow; secrets were revealed, wrongs were righted, and crops weren't planted. Who wanted to waste their time sowing crops that would never be reaped when they could flagellate themselves instead? And Pope Sylvester II, who had just been appointed earlier that year, was right in the middle of all of it.

Sylvester was a superstitious man who wasn't shy about his fear of the millennium, and he whipped his followers into a Y1K frenzy. As a result, Sylvester had a full house when he celebrated the midnight Mass on December 31, 999. He left the doors of the church open, performed a variety of religious rites, and then . . . when the clock struck midnight . . . absolutely nothing happened. Sound familiar? Well, at least in 1999 you didn't whip yourself into a bloody frenzy to cleanse yourself of your sins . . . right?

1001

NEW WORLD DÉJÀ VU

That ancient Norse ships under the command of Leif Ericsson reached some part of the Atlantic Coast of North America in the year 1001 is so fully attested in the sagas as to leave little doubt.

—The *New York Times*, November 25, 1934

When you hear the name Leif Erikson, you likely think of the strong Viking who was the first European to discover North American. (Take that, Columbus!)

What do you think of when you hear the name Bjarni Herjólfsson? Exactly . . . not much. That's too bad since Herjólfsson was actually the first Viking to spot what would later become Erikson's discovery: the New World. Herjólfsson and his crew were heading to Greenland when they were blown off course to a land none of them had ever seen before. Herjólfsson's crew wanted to stop and check things out, but Herjólfsson was a mama's boy and wanted to get to Greenland to see his parents, so he sailed on by. He knew that his discovery was important, but he suffered from a lack of follow-through and never did anything about it.

Erikson heard about Herjólfsson's story and, ten years later, decided he needed something to do, so off he went to find North America. That is why, today, Erikson is remembered as the very epitome of a kick-ass Viking hero, and Herjólfsson isn't remembered at all.

> ## ⎯ FEDERAL HOLIDAYS—VIKING STYLE ⎯
>
> In 1964, Congress signed the observance of Leif Erikson Day (every October 9) into existence as a companion to Columbus Day. Sounds like an excuse for another federal day off.

1066

GOOD THINGS COME TO THOSE WHO WAIT

[William the Conqueror] landed on the coast of Sussex, in September
1066, and soon after, in the bloody battle of Hastings, utterly defeated the
army of Harold, who was himself left dead upon the field.

—Reverend B. G. Johns, *A Short and Simple History of England*

On January 5, 1066, King Edward the Confessor slipped into a coma and died
without naming a successor. Harold Goodwinson lucked into the throne and
was crowned king one day later. But by October 1066, poor King Harold II
found himself dead in a field with an arrow in his eye. What could possibly
have gone wrong?

Turns out Harold made a few bad moves during the nine months of his
kingship, the first of which was getting on the bad side of his cousin, William
the Duke of Normandy, a.k.a. William the Conqueror. Some believe that
Edward promised William the throne after his death, and, when Harold was
crowned instead, William took matters into his own hands.

When Harold heard that William had landed in England, he wanted to
prove to his subjects that he deserved the crown. Instead of letting William
come to him, he forced his troops to march roughly 241 miles to intercept the
conqueror. In his rush, he forgot to make sure that his army was larger and
stronger than William's to tip the scales in his favor. Instead, when the two
armies met at the Battle of Hastings, they were evenly matched. But William
was persistent and, a few months later, was crowned the first Norman King of
England. Poor show, Harold. Poor show.

LOOK AT THAT DESIGN FLAW

By the time (the Leaning Tower of Pisa) was 10 percent built, everyone knew it would be a total disaster. But the investment was so big they felt compelled to go on. Since its completion, it cost a fortune to maintain and is still in danger of collapsing.

—Ken Iverson, computer scientist

You've heard the proverb about the man who builds his house on sand? Well, it seems Bonanno Pisano and the architects who laid out the building plans for the Tower of Pisa (yes, the one that leans) hadn't heard this fable before—and they're still being mocked for it centuries later.

Work began on the tower in 1173. Unfortunately, the ground under the tower was made up of clay and sand—not what you need to support a huge building. The building started to sink in 1178, when it was just three stories high. Fortunately, due to various wars and lack of funding, the tower wasn't worked on again until 100 years later. This delay let the soil settle and made the tower more stable.

The Leaning Tower of Pisa was finally completed in 1372. Over the years, there have been numerous attempts to stop the tower from leaning more than it is, but none have been entirely successful. And to think, all they had to do was build the thing on solid ground. Major fail, Pisano.

ONE SMART SHARPSHOOTER

During WWII, Nazi snipers used any tower they could find for their dirty work. To fight back the U.S. Army was demolishing all towers as they marched into Italy, and they soon found the Leaning Tower of Pisa up next on their list. Luckily, an American army sergeant recognized the historical and cultural importance of the tower and saved it from destruction.

1212

THOSE DARN KIDS!

It was not the little children that would rescue Jerusalem . . .
—Steven Runciman, author of *A History of the Crusades*

Good intentions don't always translate into good results. And the ambitions of twelve-year-old Stephen (from France) and ten-year-old Nicholas (from Germany) to conquer the Holy Land didn't really end well, either. The two, sensing that children would fare better on the Crusades than the adults, rounded up 20,000 children to join them on the voyage to the Holy Land through Italy, where the crusade began. Why hang out with your friends and chase girls when you can conquer the Holy Land? But, alas, this is where the boys' dream began to crumble.

A great number of their crusaders dropped out before leaving Italy due to exhaustion, starvation, and a shortage of chaperones for the journey. Finally, some common sense! The remaining children made their way over in seven ships, but the mission all came crashing down before they reached their destination. Two of these ships were obliterated by the rocks in rough seas, while the other five docked in Egypt and what is now Algeria where the children were all sold into slavery. So much for conquering anything.

Little Nicholas, Stephen, and their band of merry boys and girls had good intentions in wanting to do what they could to help in the Crusades. They were just years ahead of their time.

YOU SHALL PAY!

With all of these children off on a reckless voyage, the townspeople in Cologne sought out Nicholas's father—who, they believed, put Nicholas up to this—and had him hanged for his actions. Like that was going to change anything!

1282

KEEP YOUR HANDS TO YOURSELF

To the sound of the bells messengers ran through the city calling on the men
of Palermo to rise against the oppressor. At once the streets were filled with
angry armed men, crying "Death to the French" ("Moranu li Franchiski" in
the Sicilian language). Every Frenchman they met was struck down.

—Steven Runciman, *The Sicilian Vespers: A History of the Mediterranean World in the Later
Thirteenth Century*

For the majority of the thirteenth century, the Hohenstaufen family ruled
Germany and most of southern Italy (including Sicily). In 1250, the last
Hohenstaufen ruler, Frederick II, passed away. Seeing an opening, Charles of
Anjou (the brother of French king Louis IX, who would later become King
Charles I of Sicily) plotted with Pope Urban IV and took over the region in
1266, moving in thousands of French troops.

Anyone who has ever seen *The Godfather* knows that Sicilians are not
known as an even-tempered people. These Sicilians in particular simmered for
years, but everything boiled over on Easter Monday, 1282. The Sicilians were
celebrating Easter when a French solider (some say his name was Drouet)
pulled a Sicilian woman out of the crowd and felt her up without so much as
a French kiss first. The Sicilians went apes*#t and killed all the Frenchmen in
the city. Before he knew what was happening, Charles I woke up with a horse's
head in his bed, and he eventually lost Sicily. *C'est la vie*, Charles.

1348

——•◆•——

WHERE'S JIMMY HOFFA WHEN YOU NEED HIM?

[The post-plague laborers] are sluggish, they are scarce, and they are grasping. For the very little they do they demand the highest pay.

—John Gower, British landowner and poet

In 1348, England was visited by the Black Death, a plague that swept through Asia and Europe killing more than 100 million people, between 30 to 60 percent of Europe's population. Of course, the British monarchy was heartbroken about the deaths of England's citizens and did whatever they could to help the poor improve their lives . . . and if you believe that, you've got another thing coming.

The plague killed off so many laborers that, for the first time, workers were able to demand their own wages and band together for better working conditions—kind of like a union where everyone wore tunics and tights. Needless to say, the upper class wasn't at all pleased. Instead of helping the poor, King Edward III passed a series of laws designed to keep them in their place—working in the fields and homes of the wealthy.

In 1349, Edward passed the Ordinance of Labourers, which made unions illegal. Then, when no one paid attention to this ordinance, he passed the Statute of Labourers in 1351 that set a maximum wage that workers could be paid. King Scrooge's laws caused the standard of living of the working class to hit rock bottom and kept people pissed off at Britain's elite long enough to help inspire the bloody Peasant's Revolt in 1381, which started Britain on a long road to economic reform. Way to go, Edward.

1453

Istanbul, Not Constantinople

Constantinople had been for centuries the strongest bulwark of defence [sic] against Asia. The men of the West had every interest to maintain and strengthen it. Instead of doing so they virtually let loose Asia upon Europe.

—Sir Edwin Pears

The fall of Constantinople was the result of a one-month siege on the Byzantine city by the armies of the Ottoman Empire. The city was defended by 7,000 men who went up against a Turkish army of up to 200,000. Despite the Byzantines' crappy odds, they held out okay in the beginning, and, for a while, it looked like they may actually be able to pull it off. But then, human stupidity intervened and the Turks found an unlocked gate into the city that they made good use of.

Before long, the Turks poured into Constantinople and began looting and killing anyone who had taken part in the battle. As a result, the Byzantine Empire (which had been around for more than 1,000 years) fell and the Ottoman Empire expanded into Europe and Africa. And all because someone forgot to shut the door behind them. What was he, raised in an *ambar*?

THE OMEN

In the days leading up to the battle for Constantinople, there were a number of "odd" occurrences that people believed foretold the city's fall. There was a lunar eclipse (funny how these keep coming up), a thick fog that covered the city, and a red light surrounding the dome of the Hagia Sophia, the city's cathedral.

1521

THE GOD THAT TAKETH AWAY

Mutezuma [sic] came to greet us and with him some two hundred lords, all barefoot and dressed in a different costume, but also very rich in their way and more so than the others.

—Hernando Cortés's description of his encounter with Montezuma

The Aztecs were a very faithful bunch, a people who worshipped the sun and a unique being called Quetzalcoatl, a "man" that they believed could perform miracles and teach them anything they needed to know. Unfortunately, this bizarre belief led to the fall of the Aztec Empire.

Hernando Cortés directed his Spanish army toward the Aztec capital, where he was met by Montezuma, the Aztec leader, and perhaps one of the most superstitious of the Aztec people . . . which is just what you want from your fearless leader, right? Knowing of Montezuma's habits, Cortés dressed in fanciful garb in the hopes that he'd be mistaken for Quetzalcoatl. Amazingly, it worked.

Montezuma allowed Cortés and his army to enter the city and effusively showered him with anything he wanted. Little did Montezuma know that Cortés wanted what Montezuma had, and he had no problem getting it. Cortés didn't have any trouble taking over the capital, and Montezuma was reduced to the role of a jester.

The Aztec Empire and all of the gold that was in it was basically given to the Spanish army. It's pretty unbelievable that Montezuma could be so gullible and think that a god could simply walk right onto his doorstep. Montezuma and his twenty-five years of work as Aztec leader disappeared as quickly as you can say, "Quetzalcoatl!"

1533

OFF WITH HER HEAD!

And if any person will meddle of my cause, I require them to judge the best. And thus I take my leave of the world and of you all, and I heartily desire you all to pray for me. O Lord have mercy on me, to God I commend my soul.

—Anne Boleyn, on the scaffold before her execution

England's King Henry VIII loved women—a lot. But with his six wives and a veritable harem of mistresses, came trouble. In fact, the issues started before Henry had even started the marriage marathon.

Technically Henry wasn't even supposed to marry his first wife, Catherine, because she had once been married to his brother, but the pope agreed to allow the marriage and the two tied the knot in 1509. In 1522, Henry became interested in Anne Boleyn, but she refused to become involved with him unless she was queen. The plan? Annulment. But the pope wouldn't play nice, so Henry, with Anne's full-fledged support, kicked Catholicism to the curb, became the head of the Church of England, annulled his marriage to Catherine, and married Anne a few days later. But it looks like Anne didn't have her head on straight when she helped him out.

In 1536, Henry grew tired of Anne and used his power as the head of the church (which Anne helped him gain) to dissolve their marriage. Anne was tried and found guilty of adultery, incest, and disloyalty to the king. She was beheaded on May 19, 1536, and Henry remarried ten days later. See what happens when you fall head over heels for a king?

1588

COME OUT, COME OUT WHEREVER YOU ARE

When wee came right ouer against it, we let fall our Grapnel neere the shore, & sounded with a trumpet a Call, & afterwardes many familiar English tunes of Songs, and called to them friendly; but we had no answere . . .

—John White, governor of Roanoke colony

In 1587, a group of settlers landed on and settled Roanoke Island. Their first mistake? Volunteering to settle there in the first place. The original group of settlers that had tried to colonize Roanoke Island in 1585 had disappeared into thin air, likely done in by the same tribe of Native Americans whose chief they had burnt to death as punishment for stealing a silver cup.

This new group of colonists figured that the tribe had gotten the whole "Kill the colonists" out of their system. Not surprisingly, it didn't work out that way. Things started to go downhill when the tribe refused to meet with the settlers. Then, colonist George Howe was killed when he was out searching for food. Finally, they started to come to their senses and asked their governor to go to back to England and ask for backup. He did, but, when he got back three long years later (which must have seemed a lot longer to those settlers watching their backs in hostile territory), he found Roanoke Island deserted. Some speculate that the struggling colonists merged with the tribes, others believe that they all tried to return to England and died in the attempt, and still others believe they were eaten by cannibals.

We'll never know what really happened, but if you're ever asked to go colonize a place where the people who were there before you disappeared into thin air, be smart and just say no.

—⋙◆⋘—

When You Gotta Go, You Gotta Go

He lived like a sage and died like a fool.
—Tycho Brahe's self-written epitaph

So you've never heard of Tycho Brahe? Don't worry. Most people haven't. But it turns out that he did some pretty cool stuff . . . and died in a really f*#ked-up way.

Brahe was a Dutch nobleman and astronomer who worked tirelessly to detail the movement of planets and stars and to persuade other scientists that the universe was in fact changeable. He basically spent a lot of time looking up at the sky. His assistant, Johannes Kepler, later put Brahe's principals into use and developed the laws of planetary motion. Some scholars say that Kepler poisoned Brahe so he could get a hold of his research, but it's more likely that Brahe was killed by etiquette.

Brahe was at a banquet in Prague and he *really* had to use the facilities, but he felt it was rude to get up and go. So he held it. For hours and hours and hours. Those banquets can take *forever*, man. Turns out, urination is one of those things you either use or lose because when Brahe got home, he found himself unable to drain the lizard. Eleven days later the astronomer was dead of uremia. Because he refused to take a leak at the banquet, all the toxins in his urine moved in to his blood and his kidneys failed. Brahe, when you gotta go, you gotta go. I'm sure your hosts would have understood.

> ### ═══ LOST BY A NOSE ═══
> Prior to the tinkle disaster, Tycho Brahe lost his nose in a duel. The vain astronomer spent the rest of his life wearing a variety of gold, silver, and copper noses to disguise his disfigurement. Bet no one noticed those.

1605

CAUGHT RED-HANDED

> Before [the army commander's] entry into the house, he found [Guy Fawkes] standing outside, his clothes and boots on, at so dead a time of night, he decided to arrest him . . . . And then, searching the fellow whom he had taken, found three matches, and all other tools wanted to blow up the powder, ready upon him.
>
> —King James I

In 1605, things weren't going so well for England's Catholics. Under Elizabeth I, they were fined, tortured, and executed, and under her successor, James I, they were kicked out of the country and heavily fined for their faith. The solution? Blow up King James, Parliament, the Protestant aristocracy, and anyone else of importance who would be at the House of Lords (where Parliament sits) on November 5. Unfortunately, things didn't go off with a bang.

On October 26, Baron Monteagle, who had a close connection to the king, received a letter warning King James and Parliament of what came to be know as the Gunpowder Plot. On November 4, the king's men searched the House of Lords, and the whole plot blew up in the conspirator's faces when Guy Fawkes, one of the plotters, was caught red-handed guarding a large pile of firewood, matches, and thirty-six barrels of gunpowder. Under torture, Fawkes threw his coconspirators under the bus and they were all executed—and future conspirators learned that when trying to kill the king, don't leave someone behind to guard the explosives.

FORGET GOOSE BUMPS, YOU CHICKEN!

> The Snow so chilled him that he immediately fell so extremely ill, that he could not return to his Lodging . . . but went to the Earle of Arundel's house at Highgate, where they put him into . . . a damp bed that had not been layn-in . . . which gave him such a cold that in 2 or 3 days as I remember Mr Hobbes told me, he died of Suffocation.
>
> —John Aubrey, English writer

Sir Francis Bacon wasn't afraid to try new things. He was a philosopher, lawyer, writer, politician, and scientist, and he actually invented the scientific method. However, maybe he should have been more of a chicken because his last hypothesis did him in.

In April 1626, Bacon was walking in the snow when he had one of his last great light bulb moments: "Eureka! Maybe snow can freeze chicken." This may not sound like a big idea today when everyone knows that things in the freezer stay fresh longer, but these people were operating without running water, so this was a huge deal. Never one to waste time, Bacon found a chicken, stuffed it with snow, and waited for the poultry to do its thing. Unfortunately, the chicken wasn't the only thing going into a deep freeze; Bacon caught pneumonia while he was standing in the snow waiting, and he died a few days later.

Bacon's last great epiphany? "Gee. Maybe I should have worn a scarf."

DUCK, DUCK, DEATH

Between 1957 and 1958, up to 4 million people worldwide died from the avian flu, which was caused by a mutated gene in wild ducks. Who knew poultry was so savage?

1628

—◆◇◆—

THE *VASA*'S MAIDEN VOYAGE

Only God knows [why the ship sank].

—Arendt Hybertsson, chief builder

In the early 1600s, Sweden was beginning to flex its military and political strength, but it still lacked a strong naval presence. They just couldn't keep up with other countries to be considered a threat on the sea, which put a kink in their plans to become a major player in Europe. That was intended to change with the construction of the *Vasa*, which took two years to build and was supposed to be the crown jewel in their new, world-conquering fleet.

In August 1628, Sweden's King Gustavus Adolphus was anxious to see his new vessel launched. But haste makes waste, Mr. Adolphus. Despite being top-heavy and somewhat unsteady, off the ship went on its maiden voyage. The gun decks were opened to allow for a salutatory fire while heading out—a salute that never happened. Almost immediately, a gust of wind listed the ship, allowing water to enter through the open gun ports. The rushing water listed the "Next Big Thing" in Sweden's naval artillery even more, and she sank just 400 feet off shore. Any wonder why Sweden had such trouble establishing a strong naval presence?

CHLAMYDIA: SWEDEN'S NEXT "NEXT BIG THING"

In 2010, Sweden declared September 13 National Chlamydia Day in an attempt to educate the public about the sexually transmitted disease that four Swedes catch every hour. Looks like a formidable navy still isn't Sweden's top priority.

1633

You, Sir, Are Guilty of Preaching the Truth

The error of the theologians of the time, when they maintained the centrality of the Earth, was to think that our understanding of the physical world's structure was, in some way, imposed by the literal sense of Sacred Scripture . . .

—Pope John Paul II, 1992

The Roman Catholic Church versus Galileo. One thought the Earth stood still while one thought the Sun stood still. Both couldn't be right, and it was a hotly contested debate that showed just how foolish the other looked.

Because of their differing viewpoints, Galileo was ordered to stand trial for heresy for claiming that the Sun, and not the Earth, was at the center of the universe. Each claimed to be right, even though Galileo did actual research and the church was reading from a Book. The church's main focus was a book that Galileo had written the year before, titled *Dialogue Concerning the Two Chief World Systems*, where he compared the Copernican system (planets revolve around the Sun) with the Ptolemaic system (everything revolves around the Earth). The church narrow-mindedly assumed that Galileo's book only taught the Copernican theory and thus found him guilty. He was sentenced to house arrest and was unable to publish any other written works. God forbid that this man actually spread the word on how the world works! Not that a different result was really an option.

WHAT TOOK SO LONG?

Galileo's aforementioned book was on the Index of Forbidden Books for 202 years before being removed. I guess the paperwork was lost on the pope's desk somewhere.

1657

The Bad Luck Kimono

People poured out of the residential quarters, hoping to escape the rapidly spreading fire. Discarded family chests clogged street crossings . . . bridges fell, reduced to ashes.

—Asai Ryōi, seventeenth-century writer

The mid-seventeenth century in Japan was a superstitious time. In 1656, the city of Meireki (now Tokyo) had undergone a drought. The city was growing rapidly. And in 1657, three teenaged girls, each in the possession of a sinister kimono, had mysteriously passed away before they even had a chance to wear the garment.

Of course, the next logical step is to have a priest burn the f*#ker to keep it from causing any more damage. And if you're going to burn something, why not choose a day when the gentle breezes of Japan are blowing in at you with near-hurricane force? Sounds like a plan. The Japanese priest lit the match, and before he knew it, half the city was in flames. Bad luck? For sure. The fire department did their best but, like so many others, just weren't equipped to deal with the rage of the accursed kimono.

The Great Fire of Meireki raged for three days and destroyed between 60 to 70 percent of the city. It's estimated that close to 100,000 people lost their lives.

Note to Japan: Next time, be socially conscious and donate your extra clothes. It's safer for everyone involved.

LOOKS LIKE MOTHER NATURE HAD A HOT FLASH

The Peshtigo Fire, which raged in Peshtigo, Wisconsin, in 1871, is considered to be the worst fire in U.S. history. The fire, which occurred at the exact same time as the Great Chicago fire, burned over 1 million acres and killed roughly 1,500 people.

1665–1666

You Dirty Rat!

That no hogs, dogs, or cats, or tame pigeons, or conies, be suffered to be kept within any part of the city, or any swine to be or stray in the streets or lanes, but that such swine be impounded by the beadle or any other officer, and the owner punished according to the act of common-council . . .

—Daniel Defoe, *Journal of the Plague Year*

When the first victim of the Great London Plague kicked the bucket, panic ensued. (Understandably. This was seventeenth-century London, not an episode of *House*.) Multitudes of people fled the city, and those who were left behind tried any number of things to stop the plague from spreading. Infected people were barricaded into their own homes. Only people who had been granted a certificate of health were allowed to leave the city limits.

Londoners really shot themselves in the foot when their Lord Mayor (and Rat Bastard) Sir John Lawrence ordered a citywide cull of any and all cats and dogs, which were thought to spread the disease. In actuality, the plague was being spread by rats. And the only thing keeping those rats from taking over the city? You got it! Cats and dogs. When city officials killed the cats and dogs, they pretty much guaranteed that the plague would intensify, which is exactly what happened.

By the time the plague petered out in 1666, roughly 100,000 people had died and the plague had spread to France, where it continued to wipe people out. And all because someone killed man's best friend.

> **VACCINES: AN EVOLUTIONARY HICCUP**
>
> In 1952, nearly 3,000 deaths from the U.S. polio epidemic had been reported. Today, with the help of Jonas Salk's vaccine, polio has been eradicated in the United States. At least that's what the government is saying anyway.

1666

LONDON BRIDGE IS BURNING DOWN

People do all the world over cry out of the simplicity [the stupidity] of my Lord Mayor in general; and more particularly in this business of the fire, laying it all upon him.

—Samuel Pepys, British diarist

The year 1666 was a really bad one for London. The city had already been decimated by the plague, and then one Sunday night Thomas Farriner had a little incident in his bakery on Pudding Lane (yes, really). Around midnight, a fire broke out. Farriner's family (except for an unlucky chambermaid) all made it out okay. The fire department fought the fire for about an hour before deciding that the houses surrounding the now-engulfed bakery should be demo'd to keep the fire from spreading.

The neighbors weren't too happy with that option and appealed to the lord mayor of London, Sir Thomas Bloodworth, who had the authority to override the fire department. Bloodworth, who would soon have blood on his hands, took one look at the fire, scoffed that "Pish! A woman could piss it out," and walked away. By the time Charles II got around to ordering all necessary homes demolished, it was too late.

By Wednesday morning, the majority of the city had been destroyed and thousands were homeless. And all because some government asshole didn't have the balls to stand up to some selfish homeowners who ended up losing their homes anyway.

1667

JOHAN DE WITT'S LACK OF WITS

[Nutmeg] has been called "the nut that changed the world."
—William Bothwell, *Orangeville Citizen*, Aug 27, 2009

Buy low, sell high is the popular saying when trying to turn a profit in the business world. Too bad things didn't work out like that for Johan de Witt; instead, he found himself on the wrong end of perhaps the worst deal in history.

In the sixteenth and seventeenth centuries, spices were all the rage; people would do anything to get their hands on a little parsley, sage, rosemary, or thyme. But the most precious spice was probably nutmeg, a spice that was bountiful on the British-owned island of Pulau Run in Indonesia. In an effort to keep up with the Brits, Dutch explorers were also on the lookout for spicy new locations, so they enlisted the help of Henry Hudson.

Hudson was asked to navigate a passage through North America and stumbled upon an island at the mouth of the presently named Hudson River that would come to be known as Manhattan. The Dutch didn't really care about Hudson's island because they were still frantically searching for spices, so they called on Dutch statesman Johan de Witt to broker a deal with the Brits who had shown some interest. Turns out the Brits were no longer interested in keeping Pulau Run because they had figured out how easy it was to grow nutmeg (turn around now, Johan; it's a bad idea) and de Witt wanted to obtain a monopoly on nutmeg (don't do it, Johan!), so the two sides swapped islands. Yeah, he did it. De Witt wasn't aware of how easy it was to grow nutmeg, and the Brits got themselves a bountiful holding called Manhattan. And as for de Witt's monopoly? Let's just say that he did not pass go and did not collect $200.

1692

OOH, WITCHY WOMAN

That wee the standers-by could neither see nor Hear the things which thus entertained this young woman, and I hope wee never shall. . . .
—Cotton Mather, Puritan minister

The Salem Witch Trials. One of the biggest f*#k ups America has ever seen. In 1692, forty-three young girls told a group of church elders that they either were or had been approached to become witches. Historians blame the girls' accusations on a variety of things, including jealousy and a teenage need for attention. Sure, why not instigate one of the worst cases of mass hysteria because mommy and daddy are more interested in sowing corn and tilling the fields than listening to your teen angst. These witchy bitches were the original mean girls!

But the worst part of the whole thing is that everyone (including judges and ministers) actually believed that these girls were doing the village a favor by ridding it of all those pesky witches and warlocks. That's right. Adults were sent to prison (at the very best) and the gallows (at the very worst) on the word of kids ranging between the ages of four and twelve!

All in all, these kids pointed the finger at 140 men and women in Salem Village. Of those 140, nineteen people were hanged, one was pressed to death, and as many as thirteen may have died in prison. Talk about taking things just a little too far.

WHAT'S YOUR NAME AGAIN?

The judge who presided over the hearings and sentencing of those who were condemned as witches was the (dis)honorable Judge John Hathorne, none other than the great-grandfather of author Nathaniel Hawthorne, who added the "*w*" to his name to distance himself from the embarrassment of the witch trials. Not sure that worked.

1722

⟫⟩◆⟨⟪

RYE! OH, RYE!

We read that the King of Prussia ordered an exchange for sound rye of
that affected with ergot . . .

—United States Department of Agriculture, *Contagious Diseases of
Domesticated Animals*

In 943, 40,000 Frenchmen went insane, danced down the streets, and died.
In 1089, the entire village of Lorraine, France came down with the disease
and perished. And in 1722, roughly 20,000 Russians and their fearless steeds
died of the same illness. What did they die from? Ergotism, a disease caused
by eating rye that has been infected with ergot, a potent fungus that causes
insanity, gangrene, and death.

The Russian army, headed by Peter the Great, was preparing to have a go
at overthrowing the Ottoman Empire when the army ate bread made from
the infected rye that they bought from local serfs. It may have been an honest
mistake, but it was a freaking stupid one. The cause of ergotism was discovered
in 1597, and ergot-infected rye very clearly has the fungus growing on it in
place of the head of wheat, so who knows what they were thinking.

Either way, 20,000 soldiers is a ton of manpower to lose when you're
thinking of overthrowing an empire, so things didn't quite work out the way
Peter planned. Instead, he was forced to give up all his hopes and dreams and
went back to St. Petersburg in shame. Maybe he wasn't so great after all?

A FUNGUS AMONG US

Ergotism was given to women in small doses to help hasten childbirth.
Who needs an epidural when you can just eat a deadly fungus? They
were *really* into natural childbirth.

1763

Fort Whatabigfuckup

It is important for us, my brothers, that we exterminate from our lands this nation which seeks only to destroy us . . . we must all swear their destruction and wait no longer. Nothing prevents us; they are few in numbers, and we can accomplish it.

—Chief Pontiac

In 1763, various Native American tribes went to war against the British to try to drive them out of the Great Lakes region. The British tried to kill the Native Americans off in any and every way possible, including giving them blankets that had been infected with smallpox. Kind of makes it hard to be sympathetic toward what happens next.

The Native Americans had managed to take over a variety of forts, including Fort Michilimackinac, which they found pretty easy to get into. How'd they do it? Lacrosse.

Yup. That's right. The good ol' army lost a fort because they were too interested in watching a lacrosse game the Ottawa tribe was playing. Chief Pontiac had invited the army to watch, and it would have been rude to say no, right? Turns out it was a trick. (I know. Shocker.) The army was so engrossed in the game that they didn't notice the tribesmen coming closer and closer to the fort on each play. Eventually one of the players hit the ball into the fort and the rest of the team scrambled inside.

Hmm. What could possibly have happened next? Oh, right! All the soldiers were massacred.

The things men will risk to watch sports.

1776

A COLONIAL DISASTER

It is some comfort to me that I gave them previous notice.

—General James Grant

America is now known as the land of the free and the home of the brave. But it used to be called "the colonies" and might still be today if Britain hadn't made some huge mistakes during the Revolutionary War, starting with the fact that they underestimated the colonists' dedication to their cause. Britain, the most powerful nation at the time, was fighting for taxes and because they didn't want a bunch of hotheaded rebels to make them look bad. The colonists were fighting for their homes and against that whole taxation without representation thing—and they weren't going down without a fight.

Britain also royally f*#ked up when they got on France's bad side. Britain screwed France over during the Seven Years' War, and the French retaliated by supplying the Continental army with a steady stream of weapons and money and by openly recognizing the United States as a nation. As a result, Britain declared war on France, which meant they were fighting two different wars in two different locations. The saying "divide and conquer" didn't really work here.

Generals who were paying attention to the business at hand would also have helped Britain. They had many chances to demolish the colonial army but failed miserably. When General George Washington made his Christmas trip across the Delaware River to attack the Tories, the British general, Johann Rall, had actually received a letter warning him of the attack. Without reading the letter, he tucked it away in his pocket—where it was found when his body was discovered. If he had read the letter, and galvanized his troops, he could have won the battle and seriously weakened the Continental army. Guess hindsight is 20/20, huh, Britain?

1788

PARTY AT KARANSEBES! ALL ARE INVITED (B.Y.O.B.)

Turcii! Turcii!
—Austrian infantry signaling the "arrival" of the Turks

The Battle of Karansebes was supposed to be between the Austrians and Turks, but the Turks were in for quite a surprise when they showed up on September 17, 1788.

The Austrians set up camp in Karansebes (in Romania) on September 15 after a scouting mission to seek out the enemy. They encountered a group of gypsies who were more than willing to sell them booze to help ease their tired bodies (at least according to the gypsies). The Austrians complied and a party began. A short time later some more Austrian soldiers arrived and wanted in on the fun, but they were denied access to the alcohol. Major party foul. The Austrian soldiers started fighting amongst each other, one soldier fired a shot, and a full-fledged melee ensued. Between all of the shouting and noise, the troops weren't sure if the Turks (Oh yeah, those guys!) had actually showed up or not and just assumed that they had. The Austrian army pretty much spent the day firing at anything that they deemed suspicious, which, unfortunately, turned out to be their own men. By the time the Turks arrived two days later, they discovered more than 10,000 deceased and wounded Austrian soldiers. It's a shame—they missed one hell of a party!

══ AUF WIEDERSEHEN ══

Aside from this mess of the Austro-Turkish War (1787–1791), disease and illness claimed the lives of many more Austrian soldiers, including their general, Joseph II, who didn't live to see the end of the war. Bet he wished he went out with a beer in hand.

1792

THROWING CAUTION TO THE WIND

I feel sleepy, a few moments rest would do me good.
—King Gustav's last words

Sweden's King Gustav III was having a grand old time at a masquerade ball on March 16, 1792. Donning the traditional cloak and mask combo, nothing could pull him away from the fun he was having. Not even a threat to end his life.

Earlier in the evening, he was given a note that outlined specific details about a plot to assassinate him in the ballroom where the masquerade ball was to take place. Was this a serious threat? A prank? Someone fed up with kings named Gustav? In an evening where a majority of partygoers would be wearing masks, it's an eerie feeling to be out there wondering if one of those partygoers is your killer. Throwing caution to the wind, the king decided that he wanted to have a fun evening. Unfortunately, he was having too much fun. Not one but five men, dressed to the nines for the event, surrounded him while he was dancing. One of them produced a gun and fired it at the king, causing mass hysteria. The shooter escaped but was apprehended the next day, while the king lived for another thirteen days before succumbing to his injuries.

Gustav assumed the threat he received earlier in the evening to be a hoax. Guess the joke's on him. But it turns out the assassination had nothing to do with guys named Gustav. The king's successor was his son: Gustav IV.

1794

A DISHONORABLE SALUTE

One of the saluting guns on the *Jackall* was, through an oversight, loaded with round and grape shot, and this shot passed through the side of the *Lady Washington*, killing Captain Kendrick and several of his crew.

—Ralph Simpson Kuykendall, *The Hawaiian Kingdom, Volume 1*

Sea captain John Kendrick fought in the French and Indian War in 1762, threw tea overboard in the Boston Tea Party in 1773, and was in charge of the *Fanny*, one of the United States's first ships, during the Revolutionary War. Whew! When the war ended, Kendrick became an explorer who was put in charge of the *Lady Washington*.

In December 1794, the *Lady Washington* landed in Hawaii in the midst of a battle for ownership of Oahu between two warring Hawaiian chiefs: Chief Kalanikupule and Chief Kaeo. Kendrick, at the request of William Brown, the captain of another United States ship, the *Jackall*, backed Chief Kalanikupule and sent some of his crew members to help fend off Kaeo's men. The American captains' assistance helped Kalanikupule's tribe win the Battle of Kalauao. But Kendrick didn't live long enough to relish his victory.

On December 12, 1794, Brown tried to show Kendrick how much he appreciated his help with an eighteenth-century fist bump: a thirteen-gun salute fired by the *Jackall*. Too bad one of those thirteen cannons was loaded when the shots went off. The cannonball went straight through the *Lady Washington*—and straight through Captain Kendrick as well. Bet he would have settled for a simple wave....

1798

OH, FRIGATE!

It is an old saying, "the Devil's children have the Devil's luck." I cannot find, or at this moment learn, beyond vague conjecture where the French Fleet are gone to. All my ill fortune, hitherto, has proceeded from want of frigates.

—General Horatio Nelson

In 1798, Britain and France had been at war for years. Napoleon Bonaparte was trying to expand the French empire, and Britain didn't really want to give up any of the territory that they'd staked claim to. In the summer of 1798, Bonaparte decided to send a fleet to invade Egypt and then take over British-held India in an attempt to push Britain out of the conflict so he could focus on, ahem, *bigger* and better things. Britain fought back and sent a small fleet of ships commanded by General Horatio Nelson to track down Napoleon. The only problem? Nelson couldn't find him.

Nelson's ships had taken some hard knocks during a storm shortly after he set sail, and while the ships were being repaired, Napoleon dropped off the map. For months Nelson hunted Napoleon's ships but always ended up in the port that the French had just left. On June 16, 1798, Nelson heard that the French had sailed to Alexandria, Egypt, and set off in hot pursuit . . . a little too hot because he sailed so fast that he went right by the French ships in the dark. He had lost an eye in an earlier battle so maybe that kept him from seeing the French right next to him? Nelson turned around and again missed the French, who landed in Alexandria on June 29. The French stayed in Aboukir Bay in Egypt for another month before Nelson finally tracked him down and kicked his ass right back to Paris. Took him long enough.

1804

CAN'T WE ALL JUST GET ALONG?

I have resolved, if our interview is conducted in the usual manner, and it pleases God to give me the opportunity, to reserve and throw away my first fire, and I have thoughts even of reserving my second fire.

—Alexander Hamilton

In 1804, former secretary of the treasury Alexander Hamilton and Vice President Aaron Burr were having one hell of a disagreement. Hamilton launched a pretty bad smear campaign against Burr while Burr was running for governor of New York. Burr lost the race because of Hamilton's negative ads and, clearly not understanding how politics works, demanded an apology from Hamilton. Hamilton gave Burr a big "up yours" and refused to apologize for something he conveniently "didn't remember" saying. So instead of acting like grownups, Hamilton and Burr (who issued the challenge) decided to solve things by shooting at each other.

The duel took place the morning of July 11, but Hamilton had done some soul searching the night before and decided that instead of shooting Burr he would follow duel rules and "throw away his fire," which would allow him to keep his honor without killing the country's vice president. Things didn't quite work out as planned. Instead of firing a shot into the ground to let Burr know that he didn't want to fight, Hamilton fired his gun into the trees right next to Burr's head. All Burr knew was that Hamilton had fired at him, and so he returned the favor. Burr hit Hamilton in the abdomen and the VP died the next day. Looks like Hamilton should have spent a little less time writing nasty letters about Burr and a little more time brushing up on the first rule of dueling: If you don't plan to kill your opponent, let him know so he doesn't kill you.

1812

━━◆◆◆━━

NAPOLEON'S TALL ORDER

A man will fight harder for his interests than for his rights.
—Napoleon Bonaparte

In 1812, Napoleon decided it was time to "go big or go home," and so he and his massive army set out to invade Russia. Unfortunately, Napoleon didn't do much research before jumping into this one with both feet.

Napoleon met with little resistance in his first two battles on his way to the capital city of Moscow, but he met his first test in Borodino. The Russians were ill-prepared for this attack and retreated, saving their forces for later battles. Napoleon, armed with his entire army, had a golden opportunity for victory right then and there but let it slip away. Sensing that their capital city was about to be taken over, a vast majority of Russians fled and left Napoleon a welcome gift—hundreds of burning buildings. Talk about a letdown. Napoleon decided to turn around and head back. If only it were that easy.

Forced to use the same roads going out, the road conditions were extremely difficult and food supplies were virtually nonexistent. The harsh winter months took a severe toll on the French army. When they finally returned to France, only 22,000 of the estimated 420,000 made it back.

Trying to secure the last piece of his conquering pie, Napoleon assumed Russia would be a walk in the park. It was anything but.

FOOL ME ONCE . . .

Adolf Hitler tried to invade Russia 130 years after Napoleon and also found the going rough. He lost more men in Russia than in any other battle and was ill-prepared for the winter months. Moral of the story: Leave Russia alone!

1814

——◆——

Beer, Beer Everywhere

The bursting of the brew-house walls, and the fall of heavy timber,
materially contributed to aggravate the mischief, by forcing the roofs and
walls of the adjoining houses.

—The *Times*, October 19, 1814

Sir Henry Meux founded Meux's Brewery Company in 1764 and by 1785 was in the process of building one of the largest beer vats in the world. The vat stood twenty-two feet high, held 20,000 barrels of porter, and was held together by twenty-nine iron hoops. Sounds awesome! Anything that will keep the beer flowing freely sure sounds like a good thing. But all good things must come to an end, and on October 14, 1814, the party was over.

By this time the porter vat was close to thirty years old and, like a former frat guy drunk on cheap beer on alumni weekend, showing its age. A few weeks earlier the storehouse clerk, George Crick, reported a crack in one of the hoops to the vat builder but was brushed aside. The builder assumed that the other hoops would hold. He was wrong. The hoop broke and the vat exploded, taking out some smaller vats and sending a 1.3-million-liter beer tsunami screaming through the streets. A lot of people ran out to the streets with pots and vases to collect as much beer as they could (and good for them; you gotta like those who have their priorities in order!), but others weren't so lucky. The amber wave killed nine people, one of whom actually died a few days later of alcohol poisoning. But what a way to go.

1830

A NEAT SHOT OF BOURBON

France . . . falls back into revolution by the act of the government itself
. . . the legal regime is now interrupted, that of *force* has begun . . . in the
situation in which we are now placed, obedience has ceased to be a duty . . .
It is for France to judge how far its own resistance ought to extend.

—Jean-Baptiste Nicolas Armand Carrel, journalist for *Le National*

King Charles X of France came to the throne in 1824 after the death of King
Louis XVIII. With Louis's reign, the House of Bourbon (sounds great, but
wasn't really), which had been ousted during Napoleon Bonaparte's reign, was
restored, and the French Charter of 1814 (a.k.a. La Charte), a constitution
granting French subjects freedom of religion and equality no matter their
rank, was signed.

When Charles took the throne, he tried to undo much of what Louis
had done during his reign by passing a series of ridiculous laws to undermine
La Charte. In July 1830, Charles sealed his fate when he signed the July
Ordinances, which, among other things, gave Charles censorship rights over
the press. The French were less than happy with these laws and over a period
of time called "the Three Glorious Days," wiped the floor with the House of
Bourbon. When all was said and done, Charles X had been kicked off the
throne and Louis-Philippe (who would actually be kicked off the throne
during the French Revolution eighteen years later) agreed to rule France as a
constitutional monarch. Guess it took the country a few more years to become
les miserable enough to overthrow the monarchy all together.

1830

A "TRAINED" KILLER

Somehow the politician William Huskisson, at the opening of the Liverpool
to Manchester railway line in September 1830, found himself on the
track: transfixed by the steam and slowly shunting machinery, "like a man
bewildered" as one eye-witness put it . . .

—John Gardiner, in *The Victorians: An Age in Retrospect*

In the early nineteenth century the railway was a big deal. Apparently, however,
the time period's dapper gentlemen didn't realize quite how dangerous trains
could be. Yes, there's something about a thousand-pound steam locomotive
barreling down a rail that would make anyone just a little nervous today, but
it seems that, back in the day, people had to learn from experience. And on
September 15, 1830, politician William Huskisson learned the hard way.

Huskisson was excited to attend the grand opening of the Liverpool and
Manchester Railway, the world's first intercity railroad. (It was basically an
old-school version of Amtrak—only much, much slower.) Halfway through
the trip, the train stopped to watch a parade and Huskisson stepped off to go
say hello to his friend, the Duke of Wellington. Well, instead of saying hello
to the duke, Huskisson said hello to a train named the Rocket. He died a few
hours later. Maybe a little less time spent on celebrating trains and a little more
time brushing up on train safety would have been appropriate here.

> ## PARTY POOPER
>
> William Huskisson was taken to the hospital on a locomotive driven
> by "The Father of Railways," George Stephenson, who actually
> designed the Liverpool and Manchester Railway. Guess Huskisson
> cut Stephenson's celebration short.

1836

A Rude Awakening

At two o'clock of a hot afternoon, April 21, 1836, I lay sleeping in the shade of an oak tree . . . . The [Texans] surprised my camp with admirable skill, and I opened my eyes to find myself surrounded.

—Santa Anna

In 1836, the Texas revolution was raging. Texas had seceded from Mexico, and Mexico, who wasn't all that thrilled, was doing everything it could to kick Texas into submission. So far, things were going well. The Alamo had been taken, and 350 Texans had been executed in the Goliad Massacre, which is where Mexico broadcast the message that they were taking no prisoners— literally. By this point, Mexico was starting to lean back on its laurels. They were so close to victory, but it turns out they were just too tired to continue on.

On April 21, 1836, the Mexican president, Antonio de Padua María Severino López de Santa Anna y Pérez de Lebrón, a.k.a. Santa Anna, fell asleep on the job—maybe he was tired out from saying his name? The army was exhausted and was enjoying some downtime. Santa Anna knew that Texan general Sam Houston was in the area, but he apparently wasn't all that concerned. He fell asleep, and when he woke from his siesta, he found his army in the middle of what would be called the Battle of San Jacinto.

The battle lasted all of eighteen minutes, but during those eighteen minutes 730 Mexican soldiers were taken prisoner and 700 were killed. Santa Anna was found a few days later hiding in a swamp and was stripped of his presidency. Guess a battle is a bad time to get a little shuteye.

1838

✦━◆━✦

MAKING THE MOST OF THE *MOSELLE*

Such disasters have their foundation in the present mammoth evil of our country, an inordinate love of gain . . . We are not satisfied with traveling at a speed of ten miles an hour, but we must fly . . . A steamboat must establish a reputation of a few minutes 'swifter' in a hundred miles than others, before she can make fortunes fast enough to satisfy the owners.

—*Moselle* Committee of Inquiry

You've heard the American motto Faster, Higher, Stronger? No wait, that's the Olympics, but the sentiment had applied to the United States for centuries. And in 1838, it seemed that everyone had a place to go and they all wanted to get there as quickly as possible. On the Ohio River the vessel that could seemingly meet all those expectations was the *Moselle*, a 150-ton steamboat that was setting speed records left and right. Unfortunately, just twenty-eight days after it was launched, it would also set a record for being one of the most deadly steamboat disasters of all time.

The captain and co-owner of the *Moselle*, Isaac Perrin, was totally into steamboat racing, which was incredibly dangerous. Captains would try to set the best times for voyages by closing the valves on the steamboat's boilers. This allowed the steam to build up and move the ship along quickly—or blow it into smithereens, which is what happened here.

Perrin heated up the boilers and then had to stop to pick up passengers. He didn't want to lose time, so he stoked shut the steam valves expecting to rush back to port. But as soon as the *Moselle* pulled away from the dock its boilers exploded. A mere fifteen minutes later the captain and the majority of the passengers were dead and the ship had sunk up to its smokestacks.

Kind of makes you wonder where exactly Perrin went—and how long it took him to get there.

1841

—✦—

TIPPECANOE AND TYLER TOO

I wish you to understand the true principles of the government. I wish them carried out. I ask nothing more.

—William Henry Harrison's last words

Thirty-one days, twelve hours, and thirty minutes. The gestation period of a field mouse? No. The time it takes to drive cross country? Try again. The amount of time the ninth president of the United States lasted in office? Bingo!

William Henry Harrison may have been the ninth U.S. president, but he was the first to die in office. He obviously didn't last long. Harrison, at the ripe old age of sixty-seven, was the oldest president to be elected (until sixty-nine-year-old Ronald Reagan came along almost 150 years later), and he didn't want to do anything to remind the public of it. Harrison's inauguration was held on March 4, 1841, a rainy, cold, miserable day. Tough-guy Harrison chose to wear neither a hat nor a coat and stood out in the rain for more than two hours reading his speech and participating in the inaugural parade. Bad decision, prez.

He came down with a sniffle on March 26, and by April 4 (his birthday of all days), Harrison had sneezed his last sneeze.

His death threw the government into upheaval. No one had expected the death of a president so there wasn't a contingency plan for who should govern in his stead. The good news? People stopped talking about his age.

PRESIDENTIAL LIFE EXPECTANCY

In the history of the United States, eight out of forty-four presidents have died in office. William Henry Harrison died of pneumonia. Zachary Taylor died of gastroenteritis. Abraham Lincoln, James Garfield, William McKinley, and JFK were assassinated. Warren Harding had a heart attack. And FDR had a brain hemorrhage. Whatever way you figure, the odds aren't great.

1841

—●◆●—

Nothing Like a Coat of Fresh Paint

Among the passengers on board were six painters in the employ of Mr. W G Miller, of this city, who were going to Erie to paint the steamboat *Madison.* They had with them demijohns filled with spirits of turpentine and varnish, which unknown to Capt. Titus, were placed on the boiler deck directly over the boilers.

—*Milwaukee Sentinel,* August 1841

In the mid-nineteenth century, Charles M. Reed was raking in the clams from the various steamboats that he owned: the *Jefferson, Madison, Buffalo,* and *Erie.* His fleet carried passengers from Buffalo, New York, to other cities on the Great Lakes like Cleveland, Detroit, and Chicago, and on August 9, 1841, the *Erie* was scheduled to make this exact run. She had a fresh coat of paint and was carrying roughly 200 passengers, including six painters who were scheduled to paint the *Madison.* But all good things must come to an end, and that's exactly what happened to the poor *Erie.*

Those painters may have been great at what they did, but they didn't seem to understand the science of heat transfer—or the explosive properties of turpentine. They had brought their painting supplies on board and not-so-wisely decided to store a few barrels of turpentine and varnish in—of all places—the boiler room. The barrels exploded, and within minutes the *Erie* was in rough shape. Ironically, the whole situation was made worse by that brand spankin' new coat of paint and varnish that quickly burst into flames. The captain and crew couldn't get to the life preservers, and the three lifeboats capsized almost as soon as they were launched. The whole thing was a total disaster . . . all thanks to some unwisely placed turpentine. Guess this proves that you gotta watch who you hire.

1846

GOT ANY FINGER SANDWICHES?

Thank God we have all got through and the only family that did not eat human flesh . . . . Never take no cutoffs and hurry along as fast as you can.

—Virginia Reed to her cousin, Mary Keyes

The Donner Party situation is one of the most shocking stories associated with the settling of the American West. They really should have done some planning before throwing everyone in a covered wagon and heading out on a prairie joy ride across the majority of the continental United States. Instead of following the mapped-out route over the mountains and through the dessert, they decided to take the Hastings' Route, which had never been tried before. One of the party's leaders, James Reed, was actually warned by a friend to stay on the known trails, but Reed wanted to save time and decided to take the road less traveled. Big mistake. The "shortcut" took at least a month longer than it should have, and this stupid decision caused some really crappy things to happen to the members of the Donner Party, including the loss of their pack animals, getting trapped in twenty-two feet of snow, and the cannibalism of their friends and relatives. I bet no one ever invited any of the Donners to a dinner party ever again—and all because James Reed wanted to take a shortcut.

YE OLDE AMERICAN CANNIBALISM

Apparently, cannibalism has been seen a few times in the good old U. S. of A. Between 1609 and 1610, the Jamestown colonists went through a period called The Starving Time, where they dug up corpses for food. No wonder Americans are mocked for their palates.

1848

HINDSIGHT IS 20/20

The ship *Omega* . . . sailed with a general cargo and 315 passengers. She had fine weather the first fortnight, and afterwards encountered some very heavy gales, and upon her reaching the southern end of the Banks, she lost her fore-yard, main-topmast, rudder, and all her sails.

—*Examiner,* Charlottetown, March 27, 1848

In 1848, the British ship *Omega*, with its 345 passengers and crew aboard, encountered a bit of a problem out in the Atlantic. A severe storm snapped all of the ship's masts, rendering it a sitting duck out in the open water. Hoping that the grass was greener on the other side (or that the water was bluer, perhaps?), the crew on the *Omega* called upon three passing vessels to help rescue the stranded passengers. One ship fared worse than the *Omega*, capsizing in the storm and sending all 115 people on board to a watery grave. The other two vessels didn't fare much better, and seventy more people perished from a shortage of water, which was everywhere but they couldn't drink it. The one boat in this whole ordeal that made it back safely was the *Omega*, of course. With no masts and seemingly no fearless leader, the *Omega* strutted in to port clean as a whistle, but with out any passengers. Some rescue that was!

BUT AT LEAST THEY HAD PLENTY OF ALCOHOL

In November 2010, a Carnival Cruise ship lost power off the coast of Mexico, stranding some 4,500 passengers. All were safely rescued, but three passengers had to be treated for panic attacks. No word on how many people tested their luck and took advantage of the free cruise Carnival gave them for their troubles.

1853

RED MEANS STOP!

Corporations have no souls, but they have pockets, and if they cannot be reached in any other way, heavy damage should be required of them in every instance where loss of life was the result of carelessness.

—Editorial in *Railroad Record*

Green means go and red means stop. This applies whether you're driving a car on a back road or driving a train over a railroad bridge that is occasionally blocked when the drawbridge lifts to let boats pass underneath. Unfortunately, a train conductor passing through Norwalk, Connecticut, on May 6, 1853, didn't quite get the memo.

The Boston Express train was bound from New York in the early morning hours with a relief driver, Edward Tucker, who was making his third trip on this route. The third time was definitely not a charm because, for some unknown reason, he didn't pay any attention to the signal that meant the bridge was open to allow a ship to pass. He eventually noticed his mistake—400 feet from the bridge. At that point, hitting the brakes was an exercise in futility, and the train went full steam ahead into the Long Island Sound. The train folded on top of itself when it hit the water and close to fifty people lost their lives.

Tucker didn't exactly get off with just a slap on the wrist. He was arrested and charged with gross negligence. Bet he was paying attention then.

> ## RED LIGHT, GREEN LIGHT
>
> In 1864, a train carrying German and Polish immigrants en route from Quebec City to Montreal tumbled into the Richelieu River after the engineer failed to observe the stop signal a full mile before the open bridge. Talk about being asleep at the wheel!

1854

THE INCREDIBLE LIGHTNESS OF FAILURE

Our Light Brigade was annihilated by their own rashness, and by the brutality of a ferocious enemy.

—William Russell, war correspondent

In 1854, Britain (and most of Europe) was fighting Russia for the scraps of the Ottoman Empire in the Crimean War. Things had been going well, but on October 25, 1854, during the Battle of Balaclava, things went horribly downhill for the British cavalry unit known as the Light Brigade. So badly, in fact, that the Russians originally thought the Brits were drunk during the charge.

The Earl of Lucan received orders from Lord Raglan, the army commander, to stop the Russians from taking away "the guns." Which guns? Who knew. So the fearless leader Lucan guesstimated and ordered his brother-in-law, Lord Cardigan, whom he despised, to lead the cavalry straight down the middle of the fighting. Just throwing it out there, but wouldn't you think the guy in charge would do a quick double check before sending his men into the fray? Guess not.

The calvary did not fare well—roughly 118 were killed, 127 were wounded, and 60 were taken captive—and Lucan, even after he realized the mistake, didn't even try to help out. He just stayed where he was and waited for the charge's survivors to return. Many historians blame Lucan for hating his brother-in-law so much that he didn't care enough to head down to help him out, and even Raglan blamed Lucan in the November 12 edition of the *London Gazette*, saying, "From some misconception of the order to advance, the Lieutenant-General (Lucan) considered that he was bound to attack at all hazards, and he accordingly ordered Major-General the Earl of Cardigan to move forward with the Light Brigade."

Bet Lucan wasn't warmly welcomed into the Cardigan household the next time the holidays rolled around.

1857

⇒•⇐

WE SHOULD HAVE USED THE LOW-FAT OPTION!

This encouragement of high caste ritual status, however, left the government vulnerable to protest, even mutiny, whenever the sepoys detected infringement of their prerogatives.

—Thomas and Barbara Metcalf, *A Concise History of Modern India* (2nd ed)

They say the devil's in the details, and the British army had one minor detail that nearly cost them their reign in India.

It's a foregone conclusion that people aren't usually happy when their country is taken over, and in 1857, the Indians (yes, from India) weren't too happy with the British. The Indians were forced to suffer a variety of indignities from being forced to serve overseas to the lack of any kind of promotions in service, but the last straw came when Indian soldiers learned about the new rifle that they would be required to use. In order to load the ammunition, the cartridges were greased with pork fat to allow them to maneuver easier inside the rifle. Somehow the British missed the memo that Indians + pork = bad idea. Feeling mighty offended by this, the Indian soldiers rebelled en masse, seizing the capital city of Delhi and marching all throughout India in an attempt to regain control of their country.

Being heavily outnumbered, it took close to six months for the British to gain any ground. Shuttling in assistance from China and by sea around Africa— in any way they could—the British finally stopped the rebellion nearly sixteen months after it began, as their government stepped in and took control away from the British East India Company. All this to-do because of pork fat on bullet cartridges. Sometimes it's the little things that can cause the biggest problems.

A BETTER USE

Pork fat is considered an important ingredient in cooking and can be just as important as the meat. It's too good to put in bullets!

1858

—➤➤◆➤➤—

ARE YOU DAFT?

. . . it was possible to purchase arsenic as easily as Epsom Salts.
—S. W. F. Holloway, author of *Royal Pharmaceutical Society of Great Britain 1841-1991: A Political and Social History*

You'd think that, back in the day, people actually knew what was in their food. They didn't have to worry about BPA leaching into their water or trans fats being snuck into their Spotted Dick. Unfortunately, the good folks of Bradford, England, did have to worry about arsenic being snuck into their sweets.

In the nineteenth century, it was common for candy makers to add a little something extra to their hard candies to help cut the amount of sugar—an expensive substance—that they used for each batch. What they added was called "daft," which could be anything ranging from plaster to powdered limestone. Unfortunately, in 1858, pharmacist Charles Hodgson called in sick and left his dumbbell of an assistant, William Goddard, at the front desk. Goddard, who clearly had no idea what he was doing, sold candy maker Joseph Neal arsenic instead of daft. Honest mistake, right? Both were white substances. Both were kept in the pharmacy's supply closet. That's where the differences end. Obviously you don't want to be eating plaster of Paris, but it's a hell of a lot better than sucking on a hard candy spiked with a lethal dose of poison. Twenty people died of arsenic poisoning due to Goddard's error and roughly 200 became ill. Goddard actually stood trial for manslaughter but was eventually acquitted.

The Bradford sweets poisoning prompted the passage of the Pharmacy Act of 1868—and Charles Hodgson never took a sick day again.

1858

IT'S MINE . . . NO, IT'S MINE . . . NO, IT'S MINE!

[The] plentiful and low cost fuel alternative gave a second-stage boost to the country's industrial revolution. Oil's discovery at the Drake well . . . provided unprecedented mobility to Americans.

—Lee R. Forker Jr., from the *Oil Daily*

Edwin Drake stumbled into the oil industry in 1857 hoping to jump-start a new career—a career that could have been immensely profitable had he just done one little thing along the way.

In 1858, Drake discovered an alternative method for drilling oil to allow for better results. By using pipes, he could drill into the ground without collapsing the holes he had just created (bright folks, those oil drillers) and gather the oil where it was naturally stored—in the ground. This enabled him to go significantly deeper than he had before and establish several oil-producing "towns" from his discovery.

Intelligently, Drake formed a company to help extract and market the oil. Less intelligently, he failed to secure a patent for his oil-drilling device. Others took notice of what Drake had done and started drilling themselves, producing just as much oil. All of that time and energy coming up with the device that could have made him millions on the cusp of the oil craze in America? Gone to waste. No one ever said oil drillers were good businessmen. With new technology improving on his existing model, his company went under in just four years. Inventors, be warned: Whether you've invented a Flowbee or something actually useful, take the time to go ahead and get that patent.

> ## YEAH, THAT WAS ME!
> Al Gore wildly claimed to have invented the Internet, but his reasoning fell on deaf ears when he talked about how important the "rooter" (instead of router) was that Cisco created. Al, go back to your day job.

1859

TALK ABOUT A FERTILE LANDSCAPE

*The introduction of a few rabbits could do little harm
and might provide a touch of
home, in addition to a spot of hunting.*

—Thomas Austin, 1859

In 1859, Australian resident Thomas Austin thought it would be a fun idea to have a Christmas hunt on his property just west of Melbourne. For the hunt, he stocked his property with twenty-four rabbits that he had sent over from England. Just a simple game of hunting rabbits, right? Ol' Tommy—and all of Australia, for that matter—was in for a *big* surprise.

With no natural predators and Australia's fertile landscape, the rabbits flourished. Oh, and they procreated. A lot. Like rabbits, if you will. Within seven years, Austin shot more than 14,000 rabbits on his land alone as well as potential predators that the rabbits attracted, like cats and eagles. By the time the 1940s rolled around, the rabbit population had reached an estimated 800 million and the rabbits had hippity-hopped all over the country. Sounds impossible, doesn't it? Australians were throwing everything but the kitchen sink at these rabbits to control the population, including trapping, poisoning, even using ferrets to chase them into the traps.

And to think, all Thomas Austin wanted to do was hunt a couple of rabbits for fun. Now he can go anywhere and hunt as many as he wants!

BILBY OR WON'T WE?

Even folklore isn't immune from the rabbits. Australia is making a strong effort to change the traditional Easter Bunny to the Easter Bilby, in honor of the native nocturnal marsupial that vaguely resembles a rabbit. But will the kids notice?

1861

Ripley's Believe It or Not

As new forms of breech-loading and repeating rifles were brought forward from the inventors of the Northern states, most were dismissed out of hand by the chief of ordnance for the Union army, General James Wolfe Ripley.

—Kevin Dockery, *Future Weapons*

If you were heading off to war, you'd want to know that you had the most modern, most powerful, most awesome weapons of all time at your disposal, right? Apparently that wasn't the way Brigadier General James Wolfe Ripley thought when the Civil War broke out in 1861.

Union general and chief of ordnance for the Union army, Ripley basically made all the decisions regarding what weapons the boys in blue would carry—and Ripley, a veteran of the War of 1812, was old school. The Union had stocks of muskets just sitting around, so Ripley issued those to the soldiers instead of making the decision to add repeating rifles, big guns that held more than one round of ammunition, to the roster. Never mind the fact that the Confederacy was bringing out the big guns and buying repeating rifles from European nations eager to capitalize on the opportunity to make some quick cash (hope they weren't paid in Confederate dollars . . .). It's a good thing the Union was backed by the factories and industry in the North because things could have really blown up in Ripley's face otherwise. As is, many historians claim that Ripley's poor decision lengthened the Civil War up to two years—but at least they used up those old supplies of muskets. Waste not, want not!

IT'S ALL RELATIVE

John Wolfe Ripley's nephew, General Roswell S. Ripley, fought for the Confederacy during the War of Northern Aggression. Bet he had a repeating rifle.

1862

A GOOD CRAFTSMAN NEVER BLAMES HIS TOOLS

On the morning of September 19, 1862, the *New York Tribune* printed
the first report of the battle that had been fought two days earlier along
Maryland's Antietam Creek. Within hours every Northern city buzzed
with talk of the war's bloodiest day. Every city, that is, except Pittsburgh,
Pennsylvania.

—Lawrence Spinnenweber, from the *Civil War Interactive* newspaper

September 17, 1862, began as a normal day at the Allegheny Arsenal, but the
peace didn't last long.

A midafternoon explosion leveled the facility, killing seventy-eight people
and sending those that remained scrambling for answers. What could have
caused this ammunition factory to just explode? Why, a horse, of course! It is
widely believed that while barrels of gunpowder were being loaded into the
factory, some powder leaked onto the streets, causing a chain of powder that
led into the factory. Then, one of the horse's metal shoes sparked and ignited the
powder. Since when did Wile E. Coyote and his cartoon friends find work at
this factory? They seem to know a lot about lugging barrels with leaking powder.

About those barrels . . . lab superintendent Alexander McBride and Col.
John Symington deflected blame to DuPont (the company supplying the
barrels) for reusing barrels and thus creating the holes in them. Bad enough that
they allowed the powder to spill all over the ground and into the warehouse,
but to cast blame on someone else on top of it? Man up, guys.

BECAUSE OF A HORSE

Amazingly, this incident occurred on the bloodiest single day during
the Civil War, thanks to the Battle of Antietam. This incident brought
the death toll even higher . . . and all because of a one-cent nail.

1863

TROUBLE WITH COMMUNICATION

I was obliged to use wire in which I had but little confidence . . . I think that justice to the corps demands that I should here state that on the preceding day I had requested permission to abandon this line and bring in the wire for repairs, but was refused.

—Captain Samuel T. Cushing, acting chief signal officer at the Battle of Chancellorsville

During the Civil War, the Union army was looking for a way for its troops to communicate with each other when they were in the field (the whole no-cell-phone thing was a major disadvantage) and decided the Beardslee Magneto-Electric Field Telegraph Machine fit the bill. The telegraph was portable—sort of. It weighed 100 pounds and only had a seven-mile range, which meant that each machine had to be connected to other machines by wires. It was also reliable—or so they thought. Turns out there were some kinks. The wire had to be replaced frequently, and the machine was so sensitive that it only took a few hard knocks to push the letters out of whack. Not to mention the fact that setting up a heavy, awkward telegraph system on a battlefield was more than a little difficult.

The Beardslee telegraph debacle came to a head at the Battle of Chancellorsville. For starters, the army didn't have enough wire to properly run the telegraph and was forced to tap into the wires at Belle Plain, a Union outpost. Captain Samuel T. Cushing, the Union's acting chief signal officer, wanted to make sure the wires were working properly, but his request was denied due to his boss's overconfidence in the system. This, combined with the failure of the faulty wiring, an unlucky lighting strike that took out one of the machines, and the fact that the telegraph was sending garbled messages led to the Union's stunning defeat by Confederate commander Robert E. Lee. Guess nothing good comes out of being an early adopter.

1863

WAIT, WHERE ARE WE GOING?

It is my opinion that no fifteen thousand men ever arrayed for battle can take that position.

—Lt. Gen. James Longstreet, man assigned to lead Pickett's Charge

It's in bad taste to have an "I told you so" moment in war when thousands of lives are at stake. Yet that's what took place among the Confederate army in the Civil War.

General Robert E. Lee, Major General George Pickett, and Lieutenant General James Longstreet decided to launch an attack on the Union stronghold near Gettysburg, Pennsylvania. Attacks on this front by the Confederates had failed each of the prior two days, yet Lee wanted to give it a third try, hoping it was a charm. They organized an infantry assault to be paired with artillery fire that would (hopefully) wipe out the Union artillery and give the infantry an easier chance to plow through the Union line. At least, that was the plan.

Longstreet wasn't the least bit convinced this would work. Working against them was the lack of enough able soldiers, as the most tired of the bunch were ordered to lead. Also working against them was the fact that the whole thing wasn't really a "charge" but a "march" and then charge once they were close. Rather than taking a hard look at what they were working with and sending some divisions around the Union forces, the Confederates instead decided to fully penetrate the central Union line, which the Confederate army just couldn't handle. The Confederate losses outnumbered the Union losses by more than five to one.

Pickett's Charge was more like Pickett's Stand Around and Watch Us Get Annihilated.

1863

FIRE AND BRIMSTONE

This year, determined to outshine all former exhibitions, [the church curate] made arrangements to adorn the church with garlands of flowers, colossal statues, and with an unprecedented number of lights. He was vainly remonstrated with by the Archbishop and others in authority, who reluctaatly [sic] gave their consent to the display.

—The New York Times, December 14, 1863

The members of the Jesuit Church of the Company of Jesus in Santiago, Chile, loved the Virgin Mary. A lot. They celebrated for the entire month leading up to the Feast of the Immaculate Conception, but the big day itself was the apex of the year for the congregation. Unfortunately, while the church's priest loved Mary, he also really loved a spectacle—which is exactly what he got. (Guess he never took that vow of humility.)

The priest wanted this year's celebration to be better than any the church had put on before, so he decided to light up the entire building with candles and oil lamps. His higher-ups weren't thrilled, but they eventually gave in, and on December 8, 1863, the church was illuminated with close to 20,000 oil lamps. It must have been beautiful—for about ten minutes—before the church erupted in flames.

Ironically, it was one of the lamps surrounding a statue of the Virgin Mary that exploded first. A church usher tried to put the fire out with his poncho, but he only succeeded in spreading the fire to the wooden roof. To add insult to injury, the church's doors had been closed to enhance the congregation's praying pleasure and the city didn't have an organized fire department. When all was said and done, one-third of Santiago's population had been either killed or injured and the church had to be razed. Way to end the feast with a bang, Father. Amen.

1865

——◆◆——

OUR AMERICAN DISASTER

Had [John Frederick Parker] done his duty, I believe President Lincoln
would not have been murdered by Booth.

—William H. Crook, one of Lincoln's bodyguards

We all know the story of the Lincoln Assassination. Six days after Robert E.
Lee surrendered, Abraham Lincoln went to see *Our American Cousin* at Ford's
Theatre in Washington, D.C., with his wife, crazy Mary Todd Lincoln, Major
Henry R. Rathbone, and Rathbone's fiancé Clara Harris. John Wilkes Booth
snuck into Lincoln's booth, shot him, and then leapt onto the stage to escape.
Lincoln died hours later.

What you may not know is that Lincoln actually had a bodyguard that
night. John Frederick Parker was one of four men who made up the first
permanent police detail whose sole job was to guard the president. Apparently
Parker didn't read the job description.

So where was our bodyguard when Booth pulled the trigger? Drinking
at the Star Saloon with Lincoln's coachman. Nicely done. At least Parker was
man enough to admit he screwed up. Supposedly he told Mary Todd Lincoln,
"I did wrong, I admit, and have bitterly repented. I did not believe any one
would try to kill so good a man in such a public place, and the belief made me
careless." This is one mistake you can't take back, Mr. Parker.

TALK ABOUT A NIGHT TERROR

Several days before Lincoln was shot, he had a dream where he
attended his own funeral. Maybe he should have just stayed home.

1871

THAT DAMN COW!

For days past alarm has followed alarm . . . and we have forgotten that the absence of rain for three weeks has left everything in so dry and inflammable a condition that a spark might set a fire which would sweep from end to end of the city.

—*Chicago Tribune*, October 7, 1871

Let's clear one thing up right from the beginning: Catherine O'Leary's cow did not cause the Great Chicago Fire. In fact, the fire went from harmless fire to major f*#k up due to poor city planning and a fire department telegraph operator who wasn't on his game.

When the fire started on October 8, 1871, only an inch of rain had fallen since July, and Chicago itself was a major fire hazard. The *Chicago Tribune* had called for increased fire patrols for weeks, but they were ignored. In fact, a fire the day before the great fire started had destroyed four blocks of the city, which meant the firemen were exhausted and the city's water reserves were already low when the great fire started.

To make things worse, William J. Brown, the telegraph operator whose only job was to ring the appropriate alarm bells to tell the firefighters where to go, rang the wrong bell and sent the force to the wrong location. Even when he realized his mistake, Brown refused to allow the correct bells to be rung, saying that he didn't want to confuse the firemen. Hmm . . . either confuse the firemen or allow a fire that would eventually destroy roughly 17,000 buildings and leave 300,000 homeless to burn itself out? Good choice, Brown.

1876

━━◆◆◆━━

BATTLE OF LITTLE BIGHORN

The soldiers charged the Sioux camp about noon . . . these soldiers
became foolish, many throwing away their guns and raising their hands,
saying, 'Sioux, pity us; take us prisoners.' The Sioux did not take a single
soldier prisoner, but killed all of them; none were left alive for even a
few minutes.

—Red Horse, Lakota chief

When General George Armstrong Custer decided to attack a village of Native
Americans on June 25, 1876, he had no idea what he was getting himself into.
By this time the U.S. Army had been trying their best to force the Native
Americans, led by Chief Sitting Bull, back on to their designated reservations
(a series of incidents known as the Great Sioux War) for a few months now,
but Sitting Bull wasn't about to "go to his room" without a fight. Custer had his
ass handed to him by the tribe, and well he should have. He made some serious
mistakes that led to his not-so-unfortunate demise.

First, Custer refused to let his troops arm themselves with Gatling guns,
an early version of an automatic weapon that could fire a series of rounds one
after the other. Guess he didn't know that Sitting Bull's troops were sitting on
some pretty sweet repeating riflery and were just waiting for the right time to
show them off.

Custer also thought he was just going to march into a poorly protected
village, take the women and children hostage, and use them to force the
warriors to surrender. Aside from this being a total dick move, it didn't work.
The village was full of fighters, and some historians say that Custer's troops
were outnumbered three to one.

Custer's entire company was annihilated—who are we to say if they
deserved it?

1876

LET'S PLAY TELEPHONE

This electrical toy has far too many shortcomings to ever be considered a practical means of communication. This device is inherently of no value to us.

—William Orton, president of Western Union

We're all familiar with Western Union: If you're in college and you need money for books, rent, or liquor, you have someone wire you cash. If you've been caught by Dog the Bounty Hunter and need bail money, you know where to go. But back in the day, Western Union was the communications king. It put the Pony Express out of business, and by 1866 it controlled 90 percent of all telegraph lines in the United States. Then along came Alexander Graham Bell.

Bell invented the telephone in 1876 and, wanting to play nice with one of America's largest monopolies—and line the pockets of his waistcoat, of course—offered to sell the patent to Western Union for $100,000 with no strings attached. But Western Union clearly lacked foresight and the sale was a no-go. The company soon realized its f*#k up and tried to set up its own telephone system, but by 1879 it threw in the towel. Bell walked away to fame and fortune, and Western Union settled in for a future of seedy convenience stores and desperate convicts looking for their next bailout. Looks like Bell got the last laugh, something that was always hard to get across via telegraph.

1876

DYSFUNCTION JUNCTION

The night was a wild and bitter one. A furious snow-storm had raged all the previous day, and had heaped great masses of snow along and across the track. The wind was a cold, biting one, and was blowing with a velocity of about forty miles per hour. The darkness was dense. On such a night as this the train, composed of eleven coaches, and drawn by two heavy engines, approached the fated bridge, located about one thousand feet east of the Ashtabula station.

—Ashtabula County Archives

The Ashtabula River Railroad Bridge was the first bridge of its kind ever built. It was designed by Amasa Stone and Charles Collins, who wasn't 100 percent sure he believed that bridge would hold. Well, if a bridge's architect doesn't trust it, neither should you.

The train wreck that came to be known as the Ashtabula Horror happened on December 19, 1876, in Ashtabula, Ohio. The first car made it across, but then the bridge cracked, broke, and fell into the river below, taking the train with it. After the fall, the heaters and lanterns on board caused the whole train to burst into flames.

What caused the bridge to collapse? Good question. The bridge had been inspected and given the two-thumbs-up eleven days earlier by none other than our skeptical architect Collins, who was found at fault in an official inquiry done by the town: "The fall of the bridge was the result of defects and errors made in designing, constructing, and erecting it." The Lake Shore and Michigan Southern Railway was also found at fault for not providing safety heaters that shut off when they fell over. Plenty of blame to go around here.

1879

KING LEOPOLD'S HOSTILE TAKEOVER

What is now called the Democratic Republic of Congo has clearly never recovered.

—Mark Dummett, BBC correspondent

Greed trumps all. Nowhere was that more evident than in late-1800s Africa, where European nations began a land-grab free-for-all.

It all started with Belgium's King Leopold II, who was as greedy as they come. A man obsessed with establishing a fortification outside of Belgium (an obsession shared by none of his subjects), Leopold set his sights on an area in Africa in 1879 surrounding the Congo River that was significantly larger than Belgium. Once the "claim" was staked, Leopold assumed this was his own private property—as if Leopold drew the Belgian Congo card in a game of Risk and declared it his own. Once powers from Germany, France, and Britain got word of this, the game was on.

Otto von Bismarck (from Germany) negotiated his way to a couple of swatches on the southern part of Africa. France obtained just about all of northwest Africa. Unfortunately for those in Africa, it wasn't enough for those countries to throw a flag on a hill and call it a day. Exploitation of the country was needed to establish it as yours. In Leopold's case, it meant tax collectors came for money and the unnecessary evil of slavery was established. Leopold's greed for his one area of land created a continental catastrophe that lasted decades. Twenty-nine years after his foray, the Belgian parliament forced Leopold to hand his claim over to the government.

Leopold II's insane desire to call a land his own was an obsession shared by no one. Thankfully, he didn't go any farther into Africa.

THE TAY BRIDGE IS FALLING DOWN, FALLING DOWN, FALLING DOWN . . .

It was evident . . . that some serious disaster had befallen the bridge.

—Excerpt from the *Scotsman* after the collapse

The Tay Bridge in Scotland took eight years to build—and just one storm to wash it away. Thomas Bouch was commissioned to design and manage the building of the bridge. Bouch had a reputation of completing bridges that were on time and within budget—whether they passed safety standards was up for debate. The project was completed in September 1877 and at the time was the longest bridge in the world.

Mother Nature decided to change that. On December 28, 1879, as a train was crossing over the center of the bridge, the bridge simply collapsed, sending the train into the water below. There were no survivors. You may be blown away at how a bridge could possibly be, well, blown away, but, after a six-month investigation, multiple engineers found that the poor design of the bridge combined with the use of substandard materials and little to no building supervision was to blame. Case in point: Prior to the accident the maintenance inspector, Henry Noble, heard "chattering" after the bridge's initial opening, indicating that some of the joints were loose. His solution? Hammer iron pieces in between the joints to prevent the chattering. He figured as long as there was no noise, there was no problem. Eighteen months later, he was proven wrong when the Tay Bridge came falling down. Goodbye, engineering marvel. Hello, major f*#k up.

ADDING INSULT TO INJURY

Thomas Bouch's health deteriorated after the collapse of the bridge, and he died just ten months later. His son-in-law was one of the passengers in the train that went off the bridge that day. Coincidence?

1881

DANCING IN THE DARK

A disastrous conflagration, accompanied with immense loss, occurred last night in [Vienna]. During the performance at Ring Theater a lighted lamp fell on the stage, which was at once ignited.

—The *Wanganui Herald*, December 10, 1881

There's something about the holiday season that makes theatergoers happy. Whether they're seeing *The Nutcracker* (bring a pillow and a hip flask if you are) or the opera *Les Contes d'Hoffman* (okay, people in 1881 didn't know how to have fun), live theater just lets you know that Christmas is in the air—unless you were at the Ring Theater in Vienna in December of 1881. There the only thing in the air was smoke.

The fire was started by a lamplighter who was, you guessed it, lighting the gas lamps throughout the building. He apparently wasn't very good at his job because, next thing you know, the stage was on fire. Then all hell broke loose. The fire curtain that should have been lowered to stop the fire from spreading was never lowered, and in a moment of something way short of brilliance, the management shut off the gas to the building—which left hundreds of panicked people panicking in total darkness. Instead of walking (not running) to the nearest exits, people just ran—but there wasn't anywhere to go. The theater also didn't have adequate exits on the balcony level (which is where the majority were seated; the wealthy people sat on the floor level and hadn't shown up yet), which just made the whole clusterf*#k of a night out a hell of a lot worse. More than half of those in attendance eventually made it out of the inferno, but I bet the next time they didn't buy tickets for the cheap seats.

1889

DAM IT!

At 3:30 pm [civil engineer John G. Parke, Jr.] saw the dam go. It didn't break; it simply moved away downstream with the suddenness of a child's sand castle dissolved by a wave. Water thundered through the valley in a wall 30 feet high.

—The *Milwaukee Journal*

The South Fork Dam in Johnstown, Pennsylvania, was built over eleven years between 1838 and 1853 and kept Lake Conemaugh from causing any trouble. Over the years the dam had been owned by many different entities, including Henry Clay Frick who built the South Fork Hunting and Fishing Club, a private resort on the lake. Too bad Frick and his co-owners cared more about appearances than safety.

While building his high-end resort, Frick lowered the height of the dam so he could build a road over it and put in a fish screen that often clogged with debris that kept any spillover from the lake from going over the dam. He also never replaced the discharge pipes that would have allowed him to release the lake's water in a controlled manner—a previous owner had sold the discharge pipes for scrap metal years earlier. In addition, the dam had been leaking for years and had only been patched with mud and straw—apparently someone didn't read the last few pages of *The Three Little Pigs*.

On May 31, 1889, a storm that dropped between six to ten inches of rain on Johnstown caused the dam to give way. The resulting flood killed roughly 2,209 people, flattened 1,600 homes, and caused more than $17 million of property damage. We can only assume that engineers finally learned the lesson those little pigs were trying to teach them and reconstructed the dam with brick.

1896

DON'T BRING A GUN TO A KNIFE FIGHT

Italy would prefer the loss of two or three thousand men to a dishonorable retreat.

—Brigadier General Vittorio Dabormida

In 1896, Italy was raring at the bit to try and take over parts of Africa, which other European nations had been doing for years. Unfortunately for them, they just couldn't get their act together and had their asses handed to them by a group of Ethiopians that Italy had screwed over in a treaty. The battle of Adwa, a huge source of embarrassment for the Italians, was the result of their dismal lack of diplomacy.

From the beginning, the Italians were outnumbered—they had 17,700 troops going up against the Ethiopians' 75,000—but they didn't let it bother them. After all, they were Europeans. How on earth could those Africans win against even a small Italian army? Guess the Italians never heard that pride goeth before a fall.

The Italians marched at least somewhat confidently into battle, trusting in their guns and their superiority complexes and met the army of Ethiopians who were mainly armed with lances. The Ethiopians totally kicked some spaghetti-eating rear end—7,000 Italians lost their lives in the battle and Ethiopia was recognized as an independent state. The moral of the story? Don't bring a gun to a knife fight—unless you know for sure it's not going to blow up in your face.

RIGHT TO BEAR ARMS

To pour salt on the wound, as Italy retreated during the battle of Adwa, they effectively armed the Ethiopian army by leaving behind 11,000 rifles and other artillery. Oops!

1896

You Can Never Have Enough Free Beer

I met many groups of people coming back from that site and carrying the Tsar's gifts. The strange thing, though, was that not one person mentioned the catastrophe . . .

—Alexei Volkov, valet at the court of Russian czar Nicholas II

It was supposed to be a glorious occasion in Russia as Nicholas II was crowned tsar on May 14, 1896. Too glorious for some.

Four days after the election, a celebratory banquet was to take place in Khodynka Field. Several hundred thousand people showed up to celebrate as new restaurants and theaters adorned the square along with buffet setups for the distribution of gifts. These gifts included a bread roll, a sausage, pretzels, a mug, and gingerbread. Excitement filled the air—who doesn't get excited about free stuff? But that excitement quickly vanished as a rumor made its way through the crowd that there would not be enough beer and pretzels for everyone. That's the last thing the crowd wanted to hear. The intense police presence (almost 1,800 strong) did little to quell the angry crowd, and a stampede ensued, leading to multitudinous injuries and more than 1,000 deaths. And all over the rumor that there *might* not be a cup of beer and some pretzels for everybody. Bet the person who started that rumor never came forward.

BLACK HEART, BLACK FRIDAY

People stampeding around in the hope that they might get a precious item tends to happen frequently on Black Friday, where the big sales originate for the Christmas shopping season. They tend not to end up deadly, but that wasn't the case at a New York Wal-Mart in 2008 when a security guard was trampled at the entrance.

1899

FIRE SAFETY

It is said that someone in the procession saw a blaze, quitted his place in the march to tell the hotel clerks, and was treated derisively as a practical joker of the poorest quality. A few minutes later the inmates of the hotel were flying for their lives.

—Printed in the *Speaker*, March 25, 1899

The Windsor Hotel opened in 1873 and was home to some of Manhattan's elite. In the 1890s the hotel promoted itself as "the most comfortable and homelike hotel in New York." All that changed in 1899 due to a perfect storm of mistakes.

Mistake #1: The fire started when a patron flicked a lit match out of a second-story window. Apparently someone should have told this guy that only he could prevent hotel fires. The wind blew the match back into the hotel and lit the curtains on fire. Things quickly went downhill from there.

Mistake #2: The New York City St. Patrick's Day Parade was passing by the hotel when the fire started. Supposedly, someone marching in the parade saw the fire start and went to warn the hotel clerks. He was dismissed and sent on his way. Bet they wished they'd listened because just ninety minutes later all that remained of the Windsor was a smoldering mess.

In the end, roughly ninety people died and the hotel sustained damages of more than $1 million dollars—and that was in 1899. Imagine what repairs would cost now! And all this happened because some too-rich-to-care patron couldn't be bothered to blow out his match before he threw it out the window.

1903

Pay No Attention to the Lack of Fire Prevention in the Building

The richly appointed amusement palace . . . would prove as unburnable as the Titanic would prove unsinkable nine years later.

—Bob Secter, *Chicago Tribune*

Chicago's Iroquois Theater was deemed "the most beautiful theater in Chicago" by *New York Clipper* critic Walter Hill upon its opening in November 1903. That beauty only lasted one month.

The theater was billed as "absolutely fireproof" in advertisements, but that was clearly not the case to anyone that walked through the doors. What was missing? Well, just the sprinklers, alarms, fire extinguishers, and water connections of any kind. Not to mention the complete lack of telephones. But wait, there's more. The building was laden with wood trim and painted-canvas scenery, which was highly flammable. So it came as no surprise that on December 30, when a curtain ignited from an electrical short, the whole place went up in flames. With nothing to extinguish the fire, the patrons tried to flee through the doors that opened inwards, creating bottlenecks all around. Some tried to escape through the emergency exits and off the fire escapes, which were unfinished. Shocking! How did all of these problems get overlooked? By bribing the fire inspectors with free tickets for not reporting the obvious violations. Hope they didn't get to see that show they were looking forward to.

> ### DON'T BREAK THE LAW!
> It is now illegal to construct external doors that open inward, thanks to the events from the Iroquois fire and a 1908 fire in Ohio.

1904

P.S. *General Slocum*, You're Screwed

The number of lives lost from various causes during the fiscal year [of 1904] was 1,303, the largest perhaps in the history of the Service, but the number of accidents was fewer; the great loss of life being due principally to . . . the burning of the steamer *General Slocum.*

—United States Department of Commerce and Labor

On June 15, 1904, 1,342 people boarded the PS *General Slocum*, a paddle steamer, for a fun church picnic. But when you look at the ship's unfortunate history, you wonder why they even decided to go on board.

Over the course of its lifespan, the *Slocum* ran aground four different times, collided with other ships twice, and survived an onboard mutiny. How long had the *Slocum* been kicking around? That's right, thirteen lucky years. But these small-scale f*#k ups were just the beginning.

A fire started on board the *Slocum* shortly after the vessel set sail. A little boy tried to alert the ship's captain, Captain William V. Van Schaick, but he was ignored. Big mistake. If Van Schaick had just listened then, he could have steered the ship toward shore and avoided the whole thing. Instead, the crew discovered that all of the ship's safety equipment was basically useless: the fire hoses had rotted through, the lifeboats were wired to the ship and couldn't be used, and the life vests were so old that they were no longer buoyant. And to make matters worse, the ship had been painted with flammable paint. Apparently, the ship's motto was not Safety First.

More than 1,000 people died in the fire, making this the most deadly American disaster until 9/11. But the boat's owners still didn't get the picture. What was left of the *Slocum* was raised and converted into a barge—which sank during a storm in 1911. Good riddance!

1905

GROVER SHOE FACTORY EXPLOSION

[David Rockwell] took his orders in this matter from the Hartford Boiler Insurance Company, and if he overworked that boiler he did it without our knowledge. We do not even know why he used the old boiler this week instead of the newer one.

—The *New York Times*, March 21, 1905

In 1905, the small city of Brockton, Massachusetts, was filled with happy shoe makers who were eager to get to their jobs at the Grover Shoe Factory. It was late March and the factory was still pretty chilly, so every morning a boiler that fed steam heat to a series of steam radiators was lit to heat the building.

There were actually two boilers in the boiler house attached to the factory: one was new and worked really well, and the other, a backup boiler, was old and wasn't trusted by David Rockwell, the company's chief engineer. Guess which one ol' Dave lit the morning of March 20, 1905? That's right! The old boiler!

The new boiler had to be cleaned and Rockwell wanted the workers to be warm while they cobbled their shoes, so he threw caution to the wind. Around 8 A.M., a factory manager called Rockwell to tell him that the boiler was making some disturbing noises but was told that everything was fine. Which it was, if fine means exploding, which is what the boiler did as soon as the manager got off the phone.

To make things even worse, the exploding boiler took out a water tower next to the factory that proceeded to destroy half the building. In addition, the explosion caused a series of fires that ignited several barrels of naphtha, a solvent similar to gasoline, which took things to a whole other level.

So let this be a lesson to you: out with the old and in with the new. And don't bother keeping the old stuff around for a rainy day. It'll only come back to kick you in the ass—perhaps with a shoe made at the Grover Shoe Factory.

1906

MARY, MARY, QUITE CONTRARY

I was as diplomatic as possible, but I had to say I suspected her of making people sick and that I wanted specimens of her urine, feces and blood. It did not take Mary long to react to this suggestion. She seized a carving fork and advanced in my direction . . . . I felt rather lucky to escape.

—George Soper, typhoid researcher

Mary Mallon was an Irish cook who spiced up the meals she cooked for her employers with a lot more than salt and pepper. Every family she worked for came down with typhoid fever during her term of employment. I wonder if she kept getting jobs because there wasn't anyone left to give her a negative recommendation?

Eventually, George Soper, a typhoid researcher, discovered that Mary was a carrier of typhoid. Every time she didn't wash her hands properly, the typhoid germs ended up in her mashed potatoes. Mallon was placed under quarantine by the NYC health department and agreed that she would stop cooking if she were released. But apparently Typhoid Mary was born to cook because five years later she infected twenty-five people while working at a city hospital.

When all was said and done, Typhoid Mary infected at least fifty-three people with typhoid fever, three of whom died. I wonder what Mary cooked them for their last meal?

1907

TAKING BACK BRONTOSAURUS

The writer is convinced that the Apatosaur specimen is merely a young animal of the form represented in the adult by the Brontosaur specimen. . . . As the term "Apatosaurus" has priority, "Brontosaurus" will be regarded as a synonym.

—Elmer Riggs, American paleontologist

Remember Littlefoot, the brontosaurus from *The Land Before Time?* Would you be surprised to learn that a dinosaur named *brontosaurus* doesn't actually exist? It's sad but true. And we can blame nineteenth-century paleontologist Othneil Charles Marsh for the confusion.

In the late 1800s, Marsh and Edward Drinker Cope, another esteemed paleontologist, were competing to see who could discover the most new species of dinosaurs. You know what they say, "haste makes waste," and that expression certainly applies here.

In 1877, Marsh announced that he had discovered a new dinosaur that he called *apatosaurus.* Later that year, he announced another discovery of a dinosaur that he named *brontosaurus.* He was discovering new dinosaurs left and right . . . except he was really just finding the same species over and over again in varying degrees of maturity. Good job, bonehead.

Elmer Riggs, a paleontologist working out of the Field Museum in Chicago, discovered Marsh's mistake in 1903, and since the apatosaurus was the first name given to the dinosaur, it should have carried through. Too bad the public didn't agree. Even today, the majority of Americans are calling the apatosaurus by the wrong name. How embarrassing!

1908

Sometimes the Wright Thing Turns Out Wrong

> . . . I continued to push the levers, when the machine suddenly turned to the left. I reversed the levers to stop the turning and to bring the wings on a level. Quick as a flash, the machine turned down in front and started straight for the ground.
>
> —Orville Wright

A lot of people have a fear of flying, but wouldn't you feel a lot safer if you were up in the air with Orville Wright, the guy who started the whole shebang? No? Good. Because the guy who invented the plane was also the pilot during the first plane crash ever.

Orville Wright invented the plane with his brother Wilbur in 1903, and together the brothers were kitty-hawking their invention to anyone who showed even the slightest bit of interest. On September 17, the Wrights were trying to convince the U.S. Army that their planes could carry passengers, something they had to prove before the army would sign a contract. They did a few trials before the official exhibition, but during the big event the plane had some performance anxiety and couldn't keep itself up.

Orville and Lieutenant Thomas E. Selfridge were roughly 150 feet in the air when, due to a stress fracture, the plane's propeller flew off and the plane took a nose dive into the ground. Selfridge died in surgery and Orville was seriously injured. Needless to say, the brothers spent some time back at the old drawing board making some much-needed improvements before the army commissioned them to make even a paper airplane.

ALL IN THE FAMILY

Why wasn't Wilbur Wright up there in the plane with his brother? Their dad made the brothers promise to not fly together. Guess he didn't trust them, either.

1912

❦❦❦

ARE YOU GETTING A SINKING FEELING ABOUT THIS?

The ship itself, it was confidently asserted, was unsinkable, and inquirers were informed that she would reach port, under her own steam probably . . .

—The *New York Times*, April 16, 1912

Everyone knows about the sinking of the RMS *Titanic* on April 15, 1912—and if you don't, what the hell is wrong with you? Quick recap for those of you living under a rock: Unsinkable ship heads out on her maiden voyage, hits iceberg, sinks. The end. (P.S. The movie ends that way, too.) But why did 1,517 people have to die on the *Titanic*? Because there were some major mistakes that went on behind the scenes.

For starters, *Titanic* only had twenty lifeboats on board when she had the capacity for sixty-four. White Star Line, those cheap bastards who owned the *Titanic*, didn't want to spend the extra money—and didn't want the extra lifeboats to clutter up the deck. God forbid those first-class passengers not have enough room to promenade in all their finery.

Also, *Titanic* continued to fly through the water at her normal cruising speed (21 knots, or about 24 miles per hour), despite the iceberg warnings she'd been receiving all day long. The wireless operator, Jack Phillips, was so sick of hearing about icebergs that he told the operator on the nearby SS *Californian*, Cyril Furmstone Evans, to shut up. After all, who cares about icebergs when you're on an unsinkable ship?

Once the *Titanic* hit the iceberg and started to sink, the crew sent out distress calls and fired off distress rockets. The *Californian* saw the rockets, but the crew thought they were celebratory. They also weren't getting the distress calls because Evans had shut off the radio and gone to bed. Why a ship would ever turn off their radio in iceberg-infested waters, we'll never know.

The *Titanic* sank less than three hours after she hit the iceberg. Guess she wasn't unsinkable after all. See what happens when you assume?

1912

————————

THE ICE BRIDGE COMETH

The river is carefully watched for signs of break-up, for once the ice goes it goes with a rush. Woe be to any unhappy mortal carried down with it.

—Niagara Falls Guidebook, circa 1896

This is a tale of unprecedented mass stupidity. Every year, an ice bridge made up of huge, connected chunks of frozen mist and spray forms over Niagara Falls, and up until 1912, people were actually allowed to walk out onto the ice bridge. Some adventurous entrepreneurs even sold food and liquor in little shops set up on the ice. It was a regular party out there. Sounds safe, right? Well, let me just stress that this ice bridge was by no means a stable feature. The whole thing was made up of little chunks of ice that pressed up against other chunks of ice. If one chunk moved, the whole house of cards tumbled. And tumble is exactly what three tourists did on February 4, 1912.

Husband and wife, Eldridge and Clara Stanton of Toronto, and Burrell Hecock of Cleveland were out on the ice enjoying the party when the ice bridge started to buckle. The Stantons and Hecock were stranded on mini icebergs as the water started to flow again and were eventually swept off the edge of the falls. Note to self: If a humongous waterfall isn't frozen solid, don't walk on it. It's not rocket science folks, just water safety.

ONE LIFE DOWN, EIGHT TO GO

In 1901, Annie Edson Taylor became the first person to go over Niagara Falls in a barrel. Why? Who knows, but she made it out alive—and so did her cat, Iagara, who she sent over the falls five days earlier to test out her barrel. She took the term "crazy cat lady" to a whole new level.

1912

STUBBORN AS A MULE . . . OR A FRENCH INVENTOR

I want to try the experiment myself and without trickery, as I intend to prove the worth of my invention.

—Franz Reichelt, February 4, 1912, before his jump

A good inventor will understandably have faith in the idea and build of his invention. A good inventor will also understandably test his invention with successful results on nonliving subjects before putting anything or anyone at risk. Franz Reichelt was not one of these inventors.

Reichelt's pride and joy was a wearable parachute, so that airline pilots could deploy it to increase their chances of survival if they needed to eject from their aircraft (because that happens all the time?). Tests with a prototype from his fifth-floor balcony on dummies proved successful, but those prototypes weighed 150 lbs. Nothing like strapping another person on your back for a softer landing! Faced with making a lighter version proved difficult, as he was unsuccessful on all future tests. Thinking his drops were from too short a distance, Reichelt wanted to go large scale—all the way to the Eiffel Tower, where he arrived on February 4, 1912, wearing the suit. He had not garnered the approval beforehand to do this himself, but what does the law know? After an hour of arguing, they relented and let him up to his jump site 187 feet up. Suffice it to say, his invention still didn't work, as 187 feet later he hit the ground and died on impact.

If at first Franz didn't succeed, he would try, try again. When he substituted himself for the dummies he was using, was there really any surprise with the result?

1913

An Evolutionary Disaster

Part of the skull of the Piltdown man, one of the most famous fossil skulls in the world, has been declared a hoax by authorities at the British Natural History Museum.

—The *New York Times*, November 21, 1953

Supporters of creationism and evolution have been battling it out for years. And for years scientists have been searching for that missing link between man and ape. In 1912, Darwinists thought their Holy Grail had been discovered in a gravel pit in Piltdown, England. Too bad the Piltdown man was a hoax.

In fact, the skull of the Piltdown man was a mish-mash of a human skull, teeth from a chimpanzee, and the jawbone of an orangutan that had been treated with chemicals to make them look old. You'd think scientists would have figured it out when collector Charles Dawson (who said someone had given him the skull) said that the skull had been broken and he had put it back together again before handing it over. Even all the king's horses and all the king's men couldn't do something like that properly. Also, Marcel Boule, a French paleontologist, figured out that the skull was a hoax in 1915, but no one listened. Too bad. They could have saved scientists more than forty years of pointless research and scientific hypothesis on how the Piltdown man evolved. The hoax was finally disproved by a series of fluorine tests (kind of like old-school carbon dating) in 1953.

SEARCHING FOR SCAPEGOATS

Who actually perpetrated the hoax has been debated for years. Scientists and historians have blamed people from Charles Dawson to author Sir Arthur Conan Doyle. Who doesn't love a good mystery?

1914

WORLDWIDE FRENEMIES

Franz Ferdinand, the heir-apparent, "the future war lord of Europe," was assassinated on 29th June 1914, at Serajevo. Out of the murder arose the little flame which kindled the greatest war the world has known.

—*Evening Post*, November 23, 1916

World War I was known as "the war to end all wars," but it may as well have been called "the war that really didn't need to happen at all." The main catalyst for the conflict that killed more than 8 million people and lasted for roughly four years was the murder of Austrian Archduke Franz Ferdinand and his wife Sophie, the Duchess of Hohenberg, by Serbian assassins who wanted parts of Austria-Hungary to merge with Yugoslavia.

Austria-Hungary wanted revenge for the assassination and declared war on Serbia on July 28. After that, Europe divided itself up in the same way that middle-schoolers pick dodgeball teams. Russia was friends with Serbia so they became involved. Germany was friends with Austria-Hungary so they went to war. Then France became involved to protect their bestie, Russia, and the United States became involved when Germany tried to talk Mexico into fighting against the United States with them. When all was said and done, the world had broken up into two teams: the Triple Entente and the Central Powers.

And all this happened because a lowly duke was assassinated in an event that didn't really matter to the majority of the world. These countries may have fought with their friends, but it's too bad that they missed out on the benefits in this case.

1915

CARRANZO'S WILD RIDE

[Carranzo] gave as a reason for this attitude that the "reactionaries" had blown up railroad trains . . . and he could not deal with an enemy which indulged in such acts of crime and destruction.

—The *New York Times*, Aug 13, 1915

The Mexican Revolution was in full swing in January 1915 as Venustiano Carranzo and Pancho Villa overthrew the assumed leader following President Madero's assassination in 1913. Their forces continued into Mexico, where they captured the city of Guadalajara. In order to make sure his latest find was secure, Carranzo ordered the transport of the families of his troops from Colima, Mexico, (on the Pacific coast) to Guadalajara via train, which was a nice gesture. It's just too bad that Carranzo really sucked at math. The train arrived containing twenty cars, which was nowhere near enough to contain all 900 passengers. As a result, passengers were clinging to the roof and undercarriage of the train in order to make the 123-mile trip. What could be more comfortable than clinging to the undercarriage of a train for 123 miles? No one on this trip would find out. When the train encountered a steep hill and attempted to maneuver corners, passengers went flying off both the roof and undercarriage. One corner proved to be costly, as the entire train flew off the tracks and into a ravine. Less than 300 passengers survived the wreck. Even worse, when his troops learned of what happened, some of those who lost their families committed suicide.

Nice death train, Carranzo! Next time, do the math.

1915

❖

BOMB'S AWAY

Notice! Travellers intending to embark on the Atlantic voyage are reminded that a state of war exists between Germany and her allies and Great Britain and her allies; that the zone of war includes the waters adjacent to the British Isles; that, in accordance with formal notice given by the Imperial German Government, vessels flying the flag of Great Britain, or any of her allies, are liable to destruction in those waters and that travellers sailing in the war zone on the ships of Great Britain or her allies do so at their own risk.

—The German Embassy, April 22, 1915, posted next to an advertisement for the
Lusitania's return journey to Britain

In 1915, World War I was underway and Britain was taking some heat from Germany (one of the Central powers). Germany had just announced that they considered the waters surrounding Britain to be a war zone and that they would fire on any vessel flying the Union Jack. Sounds like a great time to take a cruise over to the UK, right? Well, a couple thousand people apparently didn't care that Germany had threatened to shoot them down and boarded the RMS *Lusitania* in New York on May 1, 1915. But the cruise wasn't all all-you-can-eat buffets and overly priced alcoholic beverages.

Turns out the *Lusitania* should have taken Germany's warnings a bit more seriously. Between May 5 and May 6, the German U-boat U-20 either sank or shot at least five different ships, some of which were merchant vessels flying neutral flags like the *Lusitania*. On those two days, the *Lusitania*'s captain, William Thomas Turner, had received no less than four warnings telling him to be on the lookout. But apparently Turner had balls of steel because he stayed his course and even sounded his foghorn when the ship was off the coast of Ireland. The ship was torpedoed the morning of May 6 and sank in less than twenty minutes.

Guess wartime isn't a good time for a pleasure cruise. Point taken, Germany.

1916

General Haig's "March" to Defeat

There was no decision reached on this theater of war.
—General von Steinacker, German army general

With World War I well underway in 1916, the German army was in a strong position to advance on the British Expeditionary Force near the Somme River in northern France. Enter General Sir Douglas Haig, who had been commissioned to break through those German defenses with the British troops and take control of the war. Too bad General Haig wasn't quite the man for the job.

With 750,000 men at his disposal, Haig began his charge on the morning of July 1. By the end of the day, 58,000 men had died in battle. Amazingly, Haig tried to penetrate the German defenses again the following day. And the next day. And the next day. For six straight months, Haig pressed on and basically saw a repeat performance of the first day every single time. At his best, he was able to progress all of seven miles into the German fortification—only to lose much of that ground in later battles. When it was all said and done, in those six months he lost 420,000 of his own troops, and another 620,000 German troops were killed in combat. That's over 1 million people who lost their lives just to end up back where they started. Some general he turned out to be.

1918

NATIONAL SHELL FILLING FACTORY EXPLOSION

Please accept my sincere sympathy with you all in the misfortune that has overtaken your fine Factory and in the loss of valuable lives . . . the decision to which you have all come to carry on without a break is worthy of the spirit which animates our soldiers in the field. I trust the injured are receiving every care.

—Winston Churchill, then minister of munitions

Factory production was really important for the war effort in 1919, and the Canary Girls (a group of factory workers whose skin turned yellow from the chemicals they were exposed to) felt the need for speed. These women worked at the National Shell Filling Factory in the small town of Chilwell, located in Nottinghamshire, England. During the war, they filled more than 19 million explosives (more than 50 percent of all the shells British soldiers fired during the war) with TNT, a volatile explosive.

Now, while those 19 million shells were needed, the women pretty much worked their yellow asses off. However, you can bet that they didn't really have too much training before they started throwing TNT around. Turns out that didn't really work out so well, for all involved.

On July 1, 1918, eight tons of TNT exploded, taking out the entire factory. The cause of the explosion? The volatile TNT being handled on a hot summer's day and the disintegration of safety standards as the demand for munitions increased. If only the factory managers had learned to stop and smell the coffee . . . or at least the hot TNT.

OLLY, OLLY OXEN FREE

The location of the Shell Filling Factory was kept under wraps to keep it from being targeted during the bomb raids in WWI. Nothing like an explosion of eight tons of TNT to keep things on the DL.

1918

To Evacuate or Not to Evacuate, That Is the Question

Ship Foundering on Reef. Come at Once.
—Wireless message sent from the *Princess Sophia*

On October 23, 1918, the steamship *Princess Sophia* ran aground on the top of an underwater mountain called Vanderbilt Reef off the coast of Alaska—and there it sat for two whole days. Rescuers faced a bit of a Catch-22 here. The ship was sitting on a huge rock, which meant that any ship that got close enough to her risked getting stuck, too. On top of that, the weather was horrible and there was a chance that the lifeboats would be tossed around and crushed as well. The choice the captain made was to . . . do absolutely nothing. At all. He just sat there unable to make a decision.

During the two days that the ship sat on the rock, she was surrounded by rescue vessels who were trying to figure out how to help. They finally decided to try and pull everyone off the ship with a breeches buoy, a zip line that went from one ship to another, but on October 25, the weather picked up and the *Sophia*'s Captain Locke actually told the rescue ships to leave because his ship would be fine, something he regretted just a few hours later. When Locke made his distress call, a ship named the *Cedar* headed right back out to see if she could help, but the weather was too rough to even see where the *Sophia* was, let alone pull anyone off the ship. The next morning all that was left of the *Sophia* was her mast, sticking out of the water. Maybe zip-lining in crappy weather wasn't such a bad idea after all, Captain.

> ### NOT ALL DOGS GO TO HEAVEN
> The only survivor from the *Sophia* was a little dog who swam to a nearby island when the ship sank. Looks like his doggie paddle came in handy.

1918

━━◆◆◆━━

Wrong Way on a One-Way Track

Because somebody blundered . . .

—Opening line of *Nashville Post* article on the accident

Two trains, one track. When proper right-of-way procedures aren't followed, there are no winners.

The number-four train, containing eight cars, was en route from Nashville to Memphis at 7:07 A.M., while the number-one train, containing nine cars, was coming from Memphis to Nashville and was running thirty-five minutes behind schedule. Just outside of Nashville there is a ten-mile stretch of rail where only one track was laid. It was common practice to give the right-of-way to the inbound train (in this case, the number-one train), so the conductor had to make sure the number-one train passed before proceeding onto the single-track section. The conductor decided to delegate the responsibility to the crew—how hard could it be to watch a train pass?—but upon pulling up to the two-track switchover at Shops Junction (a passenger stop), he saw that there was no written confirmation of the passing train in his log book. Further complicating matters, the signal at Shops Junction indicated the coast was clear, and they failed to check with the crew at Shops Junction to check on the number-one train's whereabouts. Train number four pressed on anyway—directly into train number one. Looks like it hadn't passed yet!

> ## TRAIN OF STEEL
>
> As a direct result of this accident, cars on passenger trains were made solely of steel instead of a mix of wood and steel. You know, in case a conductor decides to ignore the warnings and press on into another train again.

1919

REGRETTABLE REPARATIONS

Which hand, trying to put us in chains like these, would not wither? The treaty is unacceptable.

—Philipp Scheidemann, German chancellor who resigned his post after refusing to sign the treaty

The Treaty of Versailles, signed at the end of World War I, ended the war between Germany and the Allied powers. But even though it ended the war, the treaty actually set in place the events that would lead Germany (and everyone else) into the horror show that was World War II.

The treaty forced Germany to accept full responsibility for everything that had gone down during World War I, to limit the size of their armed forces, rework the country's boarders, and pay reparations (a fancy way for Germany to say, "I'm sorry I bombed your country. Let me pay for the damage.") to the nations in the Allied powers to the tune of $31.4 billion.

Seem like a bit much? The majority of Germans thought so too, and the treaty started to affect Germany almost immediately: the economy—along with Germany's self-esteem—tanked, and anyone who was an outsider or who didn't agree with the general consensus about the treaty was viewed with suspicion.

In 1933, Adolf Hitler came onto the scene and promised to kick the unpopular Treaty of Versailles to the curb—and show the world that Germany was still a force to be reckoned with. We know how that turned out . . .

Next time let's hope that our world leaders pay a little more attention to what they're doing. Nobody likes a bully.

1919

The Day the "Curse" Began

Yet [Frazee] sold [Ruth] to the lowly New York Yankees to finance one of his Broadway shows, and for sixty-eight years it has never been the same.

—Peter Vecsey, author, circa 1986

While the Red Sox's eighty-six-year drought of World Series titles began in 1918, there are plenty of reasons to believe that the "curse" may have began two years later.

At that time, the Red Sox were owned by Harry Frazee, a theater producer. But despite the great success of Frazee's team, who won two championships in his first three years (1916 and 1918), Frazee was really just a theater guy who "dabbled" in baseball—and a majority of his plays were based in New York City, which gave him strong ties to the city. He often made baseball trades for cash to help keep his theatrical productions (like the huge flop *No, No Nanette*) afloat. Needless to say, Sox fans were not thrilled—especially when Frazee dealt his star player Babe Ruth to the Yankees for $100,000 on December 26, 1919. Ruth treated the next fifteen seasons with the Yankees like batting practice, hitting home runs at an unheard-of pace and winning four World Series titles. The Red Sox finished below .500 for fifteen straight seasons and wouldn't win another World Series until 2004. Kind of makes you wish Harry Frazee had just stuck to his day job.

INSIDER TRADING

When Frazee traded Ruth to the Yankees, he had already turned down an offer from the White Sox for $60,000 and Shoeless Joe Jackson for Ruth. The Black Sox Scandal made Frazee reconsider.

1919

———◆———

SLOW AS MOLASSES

The explosion came without the slightest warning . . . . Once the low, rumbling sound was heard no one had a chance to escape. The buildings seemed to cringe up as though they were made of pasteboard.

—The *Boston Globe*, January 15, 1919

Harvard Yard. Fenway Park. Faneuil Hall. Boston has always been a sweet place to visit. But on January 15, 1919, Beantown took things a little too far.

Around lunchtime, the city literally shook in its boots when a tank holding more than 2 million gallons of molasses exploded at the Purity Distilling Company in Boston's North End, a.k.a. Candy Land. Twenty-one people were killed and 150 were injured when a fifteen-foot wave of the sweet stuff moving at roughly 35 mph swept through the city. So much for "slow as molasses."

The causes of the explosion were a poorly constructed tank that leaked so badly that it was painted brown to hide the molasses stains, a blatant lack of safety checks performed by the Willy Wonkas upstairs, and a failure to monitor the tank for carbon dioxide buildup on a day that was unseasonably warm—and only in Boston in January is 41°F considered warm. Purity Distilling was found liable for the disaster and was forced to pay out more than $1 million in damages. Welcome to "Molassachusetts," folks!

DON'T YOU LOVE THE SMELL OF MOLASSES IN THE MORNING?

An urban legend claims that you can still smell molasses in Boston's North End on a hot day. Not likely. The North End is Boston's Italian section, and it's unlikely you can smell centuries-old sweetener over the garlic oozing out of every pore in the neighborhood.

1919

THE WORLD SERIES OF GAMBLING

*Regardless of the verdict of juries, no player who throws a ball game . . .
will ever play professional baseball.*

—Kenesaw Mountain Landis, MLB commissioner in 1919

The Chicago White Sox reached the World Series for the third time as a franchise in 1919, set to face the Cincinnati Reds. Too bad not everyone on the team wanted to "play" this time around.

Gamblers were curious as to why a vast influx of money was being wagered on the Reds, making them wonder if the series could be fixed. The Reds were the better team, but not by as much as the wagers were indicating. Who would have the stones to throw the World Series? Gamblers would. Two members of the White Sox—Chick Gandil and Joseph Sullivan—had strong ties to gamblers and organized criminals, allowing easy access to put the fix on, and fix it they did. The White Sox fell behind four games to one in the best-of-nine series but won Games 6 and 7 before being bounced in the eighth game.

Late in the following season, a grand jury was summoned to investigate the eight accused White Sox players for their illicit wagers. With a major problem on their hands, the owners decided to appoint baseball's first commissioner: federal judge Landis. To say the players had no chance was the understatement of the year. All eight were banned for life.

What were they expecting by throwing the World Series? Like no one was going to notice? Gandil and Sullivan's not-so-brainy idea was a black cloud for the Black Sox.

A CURSE IN THE WORKS?

After the Black Sox Scandal, the White Sox would wait forty years before reaching the World Series again and endured an eighty-eight-year wait between World Series titles. A gambler's curse, perhaps?

1920

THE NOBLE EXPERIMENT

When Prohibition was introduced, I hoped that it would be widely
supported by public opinion and the day would soon come when the evil
effects of alcohol would be recognized. I have slowly and reluctantly come
to believe that this has not been the result.

—John D. Rockefeller Jr., American industrialist and Prohibition supporter

In October 1919, Congress passed the Eighteenth Amendment, prohibiting
the sale of alcohol. The amendment officially went into effect on January
16, 1920. Now, Congress has done a lot of stupid things over the years, but
Prohibition tops the list as one of their biggest f*#k ups.

Obviously, Congress didn't take the fact that Americans really like to drink
into account when making their final decision. They also didn't think through
everything that people would do to obtain alcohol. People stockpiled liquor
before the amendment went into effect, but afterwards people started to get
a little more creative and distilled their own gin in their bathtubs at home—
when they weren't buying moonshine from the mobsters who pretty much
terrorized the country during the 1920s. The same mobsters who served up
a gin fizz made out of deadly methyl alcohol. More than 10,000 died from
drinking badly made moonshine before the Twenty-first Amendment repealed
Prohibition in 1933. And that number doesn't even include the people who
died from incidents of gang violence.

Guess the Experiment wasn't so Noble.

1920

EAT CROW, *NEW YORK TIMES!*

That Professor Goddard, with his "chair" in Clark College and the countenancing of the Smithsonian Institution, does not know the relation of action and reaction, and of the need to have something better than a vacuum against which to react—to say that would be absurd. Of course he only seems to lack the knowledge ladled out daily in high schools.

—The *New York Times,* January 13, 1920

Today we know Robert H. Goddard as the father of modern rocketry (well, that's what NASA calls him anyway), but back in 1920 the *New York Times* called him a hack.

Goddard was a physicist and inventor who essentially came up with all the science the United States used to win the race to the moon in the 1960s.

Unfortunately, the *New York Times* didn't believe in Goddard and, in fact, openly mocked him, his theories, and his general intelligence in an article published in 1920. But in a move almost unheard of for the editorial section, the paper actually apologized to Goddard on July 17, 1969, when it said, "Further investigation and experimentation have confirmed the findings of Isaac Newton in the 17th Century and it is now definitely established that a rocket can function in a vacuum as well as in an atmosphere. The Times regrets the error."

Yeah, close to fifty years later, after man had walked on the Moon, the *New York Times* had the decency to admit that Goddard's theories were "established." Perhaps they grew tired of walking around with that egg on their face.

1927

IT'S EITHER MY WAY OR THE HIGHWAY

Any customer can have a car painted any color that he wants so long as it is black.

—Henry Ford

In today's world, if you can't keep up with the fast-improving technology and the demands of the public, you can be left behind in a hurry. Back in the 1920s, Henry Ford fell asleep at the wheel and may have missed his golden opportunity.

Ford's vision was to design a car that was affordable for the average American and could handle the rigors of driving on any road surface. Enter the Model T, a car large enough for the average family and small enough to be easily taken care of. Able to be produced off the newly developed assembly line, the cars were rolling out of the factories in record time and were purchased by the public just as quickly. Ford's approach was to get the design right—which he did—and keep it the same, under the belief that his car was the only car anyone would need. Too bad that he still felt the same way nineteen years later, when his competition was selling awesome, good-looking cars with comfort-enhanced features. Human nature being what it is, people stopped buying the old-school Model T and went shopping for a more comfortable ride down the street. Realizing that he was still stuck in Kansas while the others were visiting the Wizard, Ford stopped production on the Model T and came out with the new and improved Model A. Imagine what could have happened if Ford had made the switchover twenty years earlier.

1927

——◆·◆◆·◆——

GOT GAS?

As houses collapsed and chimneys toppled, brick, broken glass, twisted pieces of steel and other debris rained on the heads of the dazed and shaken residents who had rushed into the streets from their wrecked homes, believing that an earthquake had visited the city.

—Quoted in *The Story of Old Allegheny City* by the Pennsylvania Writer's Project

Nowadays we're pretty well versed in natural gas safety. If you smell gas, don't call 911 on your cell phone because it can cause an explosion. If you smell gas, don't light a cigarette because it can cause an explosion. Okay. We get it. Gas is flammable. Someone should have told that to the workers at the Equitable Gas Company in Pittsburgh, Pennsylvania, back in 1927.

The morning of November 14, a few gentlemen were alerted to a gas leak in the city's main gas tank (which just happened to be the largest gas tank in the world). What did they use to search for the leak? A flashlight? A canary? Nope. They used a lit blowtorch. They found the leak, but things didn't work out quite the way they planned.

In fact, surprise, surprise, the entire tank blew up, raining down fire and metal on anything and everything within a one-mile radius. Good morning, Pittsburgh!

══ HELLO? HELLO? ══

Among the houses destroyed by the explosion was one once called the "Most Haunted House in America." The house was originally owned by Charles Wright Congelier, who, along with his mistress, was murdered by his wife after she discovered their affair. After a few more murderous owners (it's starting to sound like Amityville, right?), Thomas Edison actually used the house to test a machine that he was using to try to talk with the dead.

1929

Tick, Tick, Boom . . . Boom . . . Boom . . .

In view of the extensive damage done and the suddenness of the explosions, and with many people abroad on the streets in danger from the flying iron manhole covers, it is marvelous that more were not injured.

—From the *Border Cities Star,* May 30, 1929

May 29, 1929, was just another beautiful day in the neighborhood in downtown Ottawa . . . above ground, that is.

The day's disaster began with a small explosion just outside of the city that then continued working its way down city streets, winding its way down the main line of the sewer system. Manhole covers were popping off as a result of the explosions, flying through the air and giving everyone an idea of where the sequence was moving. As if feeling explosions underneath their feet wasn't scary enough, now they had to watch above their heads, too. On this went for about half an hour, and it only stopped because the explosions hit the end of the line at the Ottawa River. It was as if someone lit a fuse at one end and witnessed the carnage weave its way through the city. In this case, the fuse turned out to be the waste oils that were willingly dumped into the sewage system by city mechanics that, when ignited with the natural methane buildup, caused the chain reaction. As if there wasn't enough s*#t in the sewers to begin with!

WATCH YOUR STEP!

In the summer of 2008, close to 150 steel manhole covers from Ottawa's city streets went missing. Due to the high price of steel, police suspected that thieves swiped them to make a quick buck. The things people will do for money.

1930

━━◆◆◆━━

WELCOME TO THE DIRTY THIRTIES

I saw drought devastation in nine states. I talked with families who had lost their wheat crop, lost their corn crop, lost their livestock, lost the water in their well, lost their garden and come through to the end of the summer without one dollar of cash resources, facing a winter without feed or food . . . .

—Franklin Delano Roosevelt

Today, we (well, farmers) know all about crop rotation, the importance of topsoil, and how a heady wind really blows things around, but back in the late nineteenth century, American farmers hadn't really figured those things out.

When large amounts of settlers moved into the Great Plains region of the United States, they had to sustain crops. And once that revelation occurred they did what money-hungry capitalists always do and got to work having their way with Mother Earth. They plowed more than 5 million acres of previously unfarmed land, burned the remnants of the crops (husks, weeds, and so on), which kept the soil from getting the nutrients it needed, and overgrazed their livestock. Too bad they didn't have a contingency plan for the drought that struck in the early 1930s.

Without any rainfall—and without the vegetation that kept the land in place—wind erosion caused huge dust storms, called black blizzards, that literally buried houses, choked livestock, contributed to the Great Depression, and sent more than 2 million Oakies on the road to find a better life. In total, more than 850 million tons of topsoil blew away, and the dust storms made it all the way to the Atlantic Ocean, covering cities such as Chicago, New York, and Washington, D.C. in clouds of dirt.

The lesson? Don't f*#k with Mother Nature because that bitch bites back.

1931

⟫⟳⟪

Tax Fraud? Really?

They can't collect legal taxes from illegal money.
—Al Capone

Murderer. Mafia boss. Tax evader?

Yup, we're talking about Al Capone. The Chicago Crime Commission's public enemy number one in 1930. The man who killed hundreds of people in horrible, bloody ways. The man who made millions of dollars by selling drugs and bootlegged liquor—and didn't pay taxes on any of it.

Capone was a smart cookie, despite not finishing up the sixth grade, but it seems that he should have stayed in school and taken some additional math classes. Why? Because in 1932, ol' Scarface was indicted for income tax evasion. The FBI couldn't find enough evidence to convict him on any of the murders he committed so they settled for the next best thing. And it worked. Capone was found guilty and was sentenced to eleven years in prison.

When he got out, the world had changed. Prohibition had been repealed, and Capone, suffering from syphilis, couldn't control his boys anymore. He died in 1947 of a heart attack. Ironic, who even knew he had one of those . . .

The lesson here? Stay in school, kids. And if you're going to live a life of crime, make sure you hire a good accountant.

LOCKDOWN, GANGSTA-STYLE

Capone spent time in some of the toughest prisons of the day: The U.S. Penitentiary in Atlanta, Alcatraz, and Eastern State Penitentiary in Philadelphia. Eastern State Penitentiary is now a creepy historic landmark that is open to the public. Check it out at *www.easternstate.org*.

1933

STRIKE A POSE

Estill felt so expansive when they brought Dillinger to Crown Point for a too brief sojourn in the county jail that he posed for pictures with an arm around John in apparently brazen show of friendship and admiration.

—The *Chicago Herald-American*

John Herbert Dillinger Jr. was a notorious American bank robber and gangster in the 1930s. As a young man, he spent time in Indiana State Prison, and, like any nice guy, he made friends with all the criminals on his cell block. After his release, he took some of these "friends" along on his crime spree, where he and his gang robbed a dozen banks and killed a dozen people.

Does he sound like the type of person you'd want to get buddy-buddy with if you had any intention of ever having a political career? No? Well, someone should have told that to Robert Estill, an Indiana prosecutor. When Dillinger was arrested in Arizona in 1933, Estill took care of extraditing Dillinger to Indiana to be tried for some of his crimes. Once Estill got Dillinger to the sheriff's office in Lake County, Indiana, where he was to be tried, the media descended on the building. One of the photographers asked Estill to pose with Dillinger, which, for some reason, he did. Dillinger returned the favor and put his arm on Estill's shoulder. The photos would resurface later on, costing Estill the Indiana governor's seat. Someone didn't think that one through.

MY BLOODY VALENTINE

John Dillinger was shot to death outside a theater in 1934. There are reports of people dipping their skirts and handkerchiefs in his blood to keep as mementos of the big day. And what mementos they are . . .

1934

Don't Touch That!

I was taught that the way of progress was neither swift nor easy.
—Madame Curie

Madame Marie Curie was passionate about physics and chemistry and was amazingly successful at both. She was the first woman to win a Nobel Prize and remains the only woman to ever win two in two different fields. She discovered polonium and radium and developed a theory of radioactivity that she used to isolate radioactive isotopes from matter. She was pretty much a brainiac. But she clearly didn't have much common sense.

She and her husband and fellow scientist, Pierre Curie, didn't seem to even try to protect themselves from the unknown materials they worked with. Unknown materials that glow in the dark certainly don't sound like something you'd want to palm with a bare hand when you go into the office.

By the 1920s, many of the Curie's colleagues who had handled radium had died of cancer, and Marie herself started to exhibit symptoms. However, Marie dug her heels in and insisted that radium poisoning wasn't the cause. In fact, she continued to work with it even after she accepted that it was deadly. Madame Curie died of leukemia in 1934—a death that could have been prevented or at least delayed if she'd shown the slightest bit of common sense.

> ### WHO DOESN'T LOVE A LIGHT SHOW
> When scientists learned how dangerous radium was, they placed photographic films between the pages of Madame Curie's research notes. The films, once developed, showed Curie's radioactive fingerprints on the pages. Good thing Curie wasn't a home invader. She'd be caught as soon as the lights went down.

1937

THE BIG BANG THEORY

And all the folks agree that this is terrible; this is one of the worst catastrophes in the world . . . It's smoke, and it's in flames now; and the frame is crashing to the ground, not quite to the mooring mast. Oh, the humanity!

—Herbert Morrison, WLS Chicago radio announcer as he watched the *Hindenburg* explode

On May 6, 1937, in what was the most interesting thing to happen in New Jersey until the arrival of MTV's *Jersey Shore*, the LZ129 *Hindenburg*, an airship, caught fire and fell from the sky at the Lakehurst Naval Air Station. Thirty-six people died, and the public's enthusiasm for airship travel dipped significantly—which isn't surprising. A flaming zeppelin falling out of the sky doesn't exactly sound like five-star travel accommodations.

The exact cause of the intensity of the fire is unknown, but many experts guesstimate that a few things happened that made things much worse than they should have been, including the fact that the airship was coated with a shiny silver paint that contained a combination of iron oxide and aluminum— both also found in rocket fuel. Nothing like coating a ship kept afloat by incredibly flammable hydrogen gas with highly flammable paint. Whoever made that mistake must have been wandering through the German equivalent of his local Home Depot and got a deal on some paint from the "returns" bin. But, in addition to the paint situation, there have been rumors that a vent was mistakenly left open that allowed the highly combustible hydrogen to leak out of the ship, which only made things worse. *Gut gemacht*, incompetent *Hindenburg* workers. *Gut gemacht.*

1937

HAPPY HOLIDAYS!

They were well-built, with good bodies and handsome features . . . . They would make fine servants . . . . With fifty men we could subjugate them all and make them do whatever we want. Let us in the name of the Holy Trinity go on sending all the slaves that can be sold.

—Christopher Columbus

"In fourteen hundred and ninety-two, Columbus sailed the ocean blue."

It sounds so benign. A nice little explorer gets lost in a storm, "discovers" a new world (which isn't actually true; go back to year 1001 and read about Viking Bjarni Herjólfsson), and makes friends with the "Indians." This is the Christopher Columbus U.S. president Franklin D. Roosevelt was thinking about when he made Columbus Day a federal holiday in 1937. Too bad, the actual Columbus was a real a-hole—a fact that all of America seems to fail to realize as they thank him for their extra day off in October.

Columbus actually worked his way through South America enslaving natives and stealing their gold and goods. On his very first voyage back to Spain, he kidnapped 500 natives (only 300 of whom made it to Spain alive) and sold them into slavery when he got back to Europe. A few years later, other European nations were sailing to the "New World" enslaving natives and opening up what would become a flourishing slave trade. Now that's something to celebrate! Thanks Columbus, and thanks FDR. Nice call on the extra holiday . . .

> ### LOOKS LIKE EVERYONE NEEDS A REALITY CHECK
> Versions of Columbus Day are celebrated worldwide: Spain celebrates Fiesta Nacional, the Bahamas celebrates Discovery Day, and Uruguay celebrates Día de las Américas. Looks like we all need a wakeup call—or an extra day off from work.

1938

Chiang Kai-shek's Spineless Decision

Changsha . . . appeared Tuesday to be doomed virtually to complete destruction by fire before the Japanese arrive.

—Quote from the *Milwaukee Journal* two days after the fire

During the Sino-Japanese War in 1938, Chinese premier Chiang Kai-shek was facing a mounting siege by the Japanese as they stormed through China. With city after city being taken over, hundreds of thousands of people (along with government facilities and industries) were fleeing to Changsha for safety. Its population nearly doubled in one fell swoop, and the city was struggling to support itself. Undaunted, the Japanese were closing in. Chiang Kai-shek was faced with a decision: fight for his city or surrender to the Japanese. Naturally, option two never crossed his mind, so the answer was easy—he'd do neither and burn the city down. Umm, okay . . . Chiang Kai-shek reasoned that if his city couldn't be protected, he wasn't going to let the Japanese have it, so he organized an arson team to burn the whole place down. That's showing confidence in your people! Instead of having a backbone and offering up some kind of defense, 90 percent of the city was burned to the ground, including all hospitals, at an estimated $1 billion cost to the city. I'm sure the Japanese were disappointed. All it did was give them a free path to their next destination.

> ## LOTS TO DO IN CHANGSHA
>
> The Japanese failed to seize Changsha in three other attempts (1939, 1941, and 1942), and by the time Japan did succeed in 1944, the city wasn't deemed strategically important to hold. Maybe Chiang Kai-shek should have held more faith in his people!

1939

⊰►◆◄⊱

YE OLDE LINE OF DEFENSE

Like all Frenchmen, Maginot was profoundly devoted to peace, but he considered that France unarmed was exposed to aggressions which would imperil not only France's existence but the stability of Europe.

—Pierre Laval, French foreign minister

In the time leading up to World War II, the French had plenty of time to learn their lesson from World War I and assemble a winning strategy. Dusting off the blueprints from twenty-one years earlier probably wasn't a good start.

Opting to go with a more defensive game plan this time around, the French began construction on the Maginot Line, an attempt at a fortification to better defend against the Germans. They would construct a variety of machine-gun posts, forts, and obstacles along their border with Germany and Italy, but Belgium (a neutral country) objected to such a fortification. Rudely, the French altered their plan by keeping the Belgium border open to entice Germany to enter there instead of through the fortified area so they could sweep in and attack them. Yes, you read that correctly. An Adolf Hitler-led German army was going to be enticed to enter a defenseless border to a country. In case Maginot and the French were asleep at the wheel, Hitler didn't need to be enticed to do anything. Through Belgium and into France they went, and once they were there the weapons and defenses on the Maginot Line were useless as they were facing the wrong way. The Germans had little trouble gaining control of France once they entered.

Back to the drawing board for the French.

> ## ONE BIG WASTE OF SPACE
> Not only did the Maginot Line not serve its purpose during the war, there was very little use for it after the war and it was abandoned just twenty-five years later. At least it looks nice . . .

1939

THE THROWS OF THE *THETIS*

Naval experts hurried preparations to cut holes in the fin-like tail of the *Thetis*, glinting above the surface, while her nose lay in the mud.

—The *Evening Independent*, June 2, 1939

In June 1939, the HMS *Thetis*, a submarine, was undergoing the last of her trial runs before being put into service by the British navy. Everything was set to go. Everyone was on board, the hatch was shut, and then . . . nothing. The sub wouldn't dive.

The torpedo officer, Lieutenant Frederick Woods, went to check things out, and that's where the trouble started. Submarines have openings in them so they can shoot torpedoes at other submarines or ships. And each opening has a rear or interior door where sailors load the torpedo from inside the sub and an outer door that allows it to fire out into the ocean. Obviously, you'd want at least one set of those doors to be closed before you dive to the bottom of the ocean in a tin tube. But that's not what happened here.

Submarines have something called a *test cock* that allows sailors to check to make sure the outer doors are closed: if the door is open, water will trickle in; if it's not, it won't. To make sure the test cock is clear, each vessel is given a *pricker* to clear the hole of any debris. But in this case, a thin layer of enamel paint cockblocked the test chamber and the seaman didn't even try to use his pricker. So when the *Thetis* went to dive, her front end flooded with water and dropped into the ocean floor, leaving her ass in the air and her bow buried in several feet of mud. Sounds more like a sex move gone wrong than a deadly disaster.

The rescue took more than twenty hours and only four men made it out alive—and all because of a speck of misplaced paint and a guy who couldn't figure out how to use his equipment.

1940

A Thrill Ride Over Puget Sound

Just as I drove past the towers, the bridge began to sway violently from side to side. Before I realized it, the tilt became so violent that I lost control of the car.

—Leonard Coatsworth, newspaper editor

The Tacoma Narrows Bridge was a marvel upon completion, serving as the third-longest suspension bridge in the world. How it collapsed was also a marvel.

Efforts to keep costs down to build the bridge resulted in some crucial flaws in its design. Most important was the use of eight-foot-deep plate girders to stiffen the bridge as opposed to the twenty-five-foot-deep trusses that were recommended by the Washington Toll Bridge Authority. Talk about cheap! The result of the penny-pinching was that the bridge would rise and fall in a swaying motion in varying heights across its middle section during mild winds—a sensation that even the construction workers felt while they built it. And they decided to not tell anyone because . . . ?

A mere four months after its opening, the aforementioned wave effect (called aeroelastic flutter) took hold in a 40 mph wind, resulting in violent turbulence. Leonard Coatsworth was attempting to cross the bridge in his car but was forced to get out and walk/crawl/bounce to the other side. He made it safely, and shortly afterwards the bridge—with his car still on it—fell into Puget Sound. Thankfully, the mishap only involved one car.

1941

A Date Which Lives in Infamy

We won a great tactical victory at Pearl Harbor and thereby lost the war.
—Japanese admiral Hara Tadaichi

On December 7, 1941, a date U.S. president Franklin D. Roosevelt said would "live in infamy," Japan made a really bad decision and attacked the U.S. naval base at Pearl Harbor, Hawaii. The attack killed more than 2,000 U.S. soldiers, destroyed 188 planes, and sank four battleships. It also made America really angry.

At the time, World War II was raging in Europe, and Japan (who had allied itself with Nazi Germany) was planning on attacking several European-held territories in Southeast Asia. They felt that the United States wouldn't take kindly to those invasions and decided to cut to the chase and take the United States out of the war before they even got involved. But things didn't go quite as planned.

Despite all the damage the attack caused, Japan hadn't damaged enough of the U.S. Navy's aircraft carriers or submarines, which were put to good use stopping Japan's advance. Instead of incapacitating the U.S. Navy and scaring the country into submission, the United States declared war on Japan the very next day and became a major force for the remainder of World War II. In fact, the United States came out of World War II smelling like roses and earning the title of "superpower." Japan, on the other hand, surrendered to the United States on September 2, 1945. Guess they didn't think this one through.

KICK A GINGER DAY

Japan f*#ked up again when they allowed the American fast-food chain Wendy's to open restaurants there. The Japanese didn't think a square Wendy's burger was "waaay better than fast food," and all seventy-one locations were shut down in 2009.

1942

How Much? For What? Pfffft!

*The activities of the government seem to suggest that whatever food grains
may be available will be kept in the greater Calcutta area and the rest of the
province will be left to its own tragic fate.*

—M. H. Ispahani, friend of Huseyn Suhrawardy

Chiang Kai-shek (remember him?) and Huseyn Suhrawardy both had their
methods of preventing the Japanese from getting what they were seeking in
war. If it's even possible, Suhrawardy managed to top what Kai-shek did.

In 1942, during World War II, the Japanese had captured Burma, a country
northwest of India. Sensing a Japanese surge into the Bengal region of India,
British forces—controlled by India and led by Suhrawardy—opted to divert
"essential items" out of the Bengal region and into the more fortified capital
city of Calcutta, with rice being the main "export." So Japan is just going to
turn around if there's no rice in the Bengal region? Actually, that's exactly what
happened. But the plan didn't exactly work out.

With the hoarding of rice centralized in Calcutta, citizens in the poorer
regions flocked there hoping to buy it—if they could afford it. The rising
demand led to even higher prices, and those who couldn't afford it paid with
their lives—4–5 million lives, in fact, in a self-controlled famine. Not that the
government cared. The rice was worth so much more in this new system that
they were raking it in left and right, which is exactly what Suhrawardy wanted.

Money talks, and in this case it told the poor citizens of India to f*#k off.

1944

THE DAY THE CLOWNS CRIED

*I remember somebody yelling and seeing a big ball of fire near the top of
the tent. And this ball of fire just got bigger and bigger and bigger.*

—Maureen Krekian, survivor

The Greatest Show on Earth—the Ringling Bros. Circus—was in Hartford,
Connecticut, on July 6, 1944, as close to 9,000 circusgoers were enjoying the
high-flying routines. Everything was going as planned until the band struck
up "Stars and Stripes Forever," which is a distress signal to circus personnel.
How patriotic! The distress signal was over a small fire that was believed to
have been set by an arsonist along the wall of the tent. But this wasn't going to
be just a small fire . . . not when the circus tent was coated in 1,800 pounds of
paraffin wax that was dissolved in 6,000 gallons of gasoline—all to waterproof
the tent. This works great, until a fire happens and you need water. That's a
scene for a show that no one wants to be a part of. It took just eight minutes for
the tent to collapse with a large majority of the spectators trapped inside as the
fiery, waxy interior crumbled around the inside. Spectators did everything they
could in the limited time they had to try to escape by fleeing out the chutes
used for the animals and leaping from the balconies, but it wasn't enough and
close to 170 spectators died. The next day, five circus officials were charged
with involuntary manslaughter. When the big top becomes a big fireball, it's
a big problem.

AND NOW, FOR AN ENCORE . . .

It took thirty years before the circus came back to Connecticut, as laws
were put in place making big tops illegal in the state. The last big top
used by Ringling Bros. was in 1956 in Pennsylvania.

1944

~~◆~~

HANDLE WITH CARE

People as far away as the East Oakland residential area felt the blast and were roused from their beds. Some said it felt like an earthquake, but most agreed at the moment that it was an explosion. They rolled out in their night clothes and shouted back and forth across the streets when they were unable to reach telephone operators.

—The *Oakland Tribune*

On July 17, 1944, 320 soldiers were loading weaponry onto ships bound for the South Pacific. Unfortunately, none of these men had been trained to handle the dangerous explosives and, in fact, had been told that the majority of the weaponry wasn't live. In addition, the loading winch was broken. The officers responsible for getting that ammunition loaded didn't care; they wanted it done fast and were betting on speed competitions on which group could get their cargo holds filled first. Hey, work has to be fun, right?

At 10:18 P.M., the whole dock blew up and took the SS *E. A. Bryan* and the SS *Quinalt Victory* with it. The explosion was felt as far away as Nevada and registered a 3.4 on the earthquake-measuring Richter scale. Now, who could have seen that coming?

After the explosion, a number of safety measures for the loading and unloading of munitions were put into place, but too little, too late. Looks like those gambling loadings officers should have folded their hands and walked away from the table just a little bit earlier.

NOT-SO-FRIENDLY FIRE

In the Port Chicago explosion, 320 men died. Of that number, 202 killed were African-American soldiers. That was 15 percent of the total number of African-American soldiers killed during the entirety of WWII. Not sure that counts as friendly fire.

1944

HAWAII UH-OH

Later testimony before a secret Navy board of inquiry described how every available space on every LSTs was crammed with 50-gallon fuel drums, grenades and ammo. Welders had worked on some of the ships that morning, and while smoking was barred, enforcement was lax, survivors testified.

—Hawaii Reporter

By 1944, the United States was firmly entrenched in World War II, and they were dealing with the pesky problem of the Japanese occupation of the Mariana Islands—including Guam, held by the United States since 1898 but captured by Japan hours after the attack on Pearl Harbor.

The United States wanted Guam back and Operation Forager was born. Pearl Harbor was the staging zone for the attack, and twenty-nine Landing Ship Tanks (LSTs), boats made for beach landings, were stocked with hundreds of pounds of weapons, gasoline, and explosives. However, the navy decided that there was some ammo that had been accidentally loaded that they didn't want to use, so they had members of the 29th Chemical Decontamination Company offloading the explosives. Now, these soldiers were trained to decontaminate equipment used in chemical warfare, not handle explosives— and it showed. The men were smoking, a big no-no, and there's a chance that some of the explosives were dropped, causing a fireball so big that the base burned for twenty-four hours straight and up to 392 men were killed.

To hush up the whole thing, the U.S. Navy hauled the top secret wreckage from the explosion out to sea and dumped it so no one would know what happened. Records on the incident weren't released until 1960. Way to fess up to your f*#k up, America!

1945

Whoa . . . When Did THAT Get There?

At the present time, I can't see the top of the Empire State Building.
—Last words from air traffic controller to Col. William Smith, B-25 bomber pilot

The Empire State Building, the largest building in the world in 1945, is a really, REALLY hard structure to miss. Try telling that to Col. William Smith and the other military pilots on the morning of Saturday, July 28.

A heavy fog was hanging over the Manhattan area, making a landing at New York's LaGuardia Airport a bit of a challenge. Smith requested to land his B-25 bomber plane in Newark, New Jersey, instead, which was granted. Flying low in the heavy fog, Smith somehow managed to forget about the really large Empire State Building that was in his flight path. Must have been some really dense fog! Smith tried to pull up over the building, but he was too late. The plane crashed through the seventy-eighth and seventy-ninth floors, through the offices of the National Catholic Welfare Conference where a staff of fifteen people were hoping to get some catch-up work done on the weekend. Eleven of the fifteen workers plus all three military men in the plane perished in the crash.

You'd think Smith would have had a breeze with this journey, having been in the cockpit for much nastier missions around the world. Avoiding enemy gunfire is tough, but the Empire State Building was too much of a match for this pilot.

DÉJÀ VU

Just ten months later, a U.S. Air Force C-45 Beechcraft plane headed for Newark, New Jersey, crashed into the fifty-eighth floor of the Trump Building on Wall Street. Fog and poor visibility were to blame. Mother Nature was right up there among our greatest enemies in air combat.

1945

S*#T Happens

The call of nature is a fact of life that must be dealt with by the designer of every war vehicle that requires manning. On a ship, it's easy—there's always the sea. In a small plane, you might have to hold on but no flight can last more than a few hours. A submarine is more problematic.

—Published in the *Independent*, a UK newspaper, August 2008

Ah, Nazi Germany. You made so many mistakes that were too horrible to even include in this book, but luckily you left us a gem when you made Kptlt. Karl-Adolf Schlitt, the commander of U-1206, a state-of-the-art submarine.

In March 1945, U-1206 was fitted with a new plumbing system that would allow the crew to do things deep under the sea that they'd never done before, namely, poop. This new toilet system was a wee bit too complicated for the average sailor, so each sub had one guy who was trained to, well, flush. It was a crappy job, but it turned out to be an important one.

On April 14, the submarine was gliding at maximum depth, and Schlitt needed to use the facilities. Once he had taken care of business, he decided that he was smart enough to flush the toilet on his own. He read the manual and flushed. What happened next? The U-boat flooded and was forced to surface . . . right into the bull's-eye of a British Coastal Command aircraft that promptly bombed the sub. Oops! Once word of the sinking got out, the term "taking a Schlitt" took on a whole new meaning.

1945

The USS Wherethellisit

No evidence has been developed that any distress message from the ship was received by any ship, aircraft or shore station.
—From Navy Department Press Release, February 23, 1946

The USS *Indianapolis* embarked on a route from Guam to the Phillipines where, on July 30, it was hit with two torpedoes from an undetected Japanese submarine. The unnecessary nightmare that the men on board would go through was about to begin.

The men that survived the initial sinking began to wait for some form of rescue, thinking the navy would be there soon ... and they would have, had they known that the ship had sunk. How could that have happened, you ask? Three separate stations received the distress signals radioed from the *Indianapolis*, and each commander had a separate story: one was drunk, another asked not to be disturbed, and the last thought it was a Japanese prank. (Because the Japanese were known as pranksters back in the 1940s?) How lame is that! On top of the "missed" distress signals, the port commanders assumed that the *Indianapolis* had already reached its destination because they assumed ships that large aren't late. Well, you know what happens when you assume.

The remaining soldiers were left adrift in the ocean for three and a half days before a pilot spotted them in the water. Only 316 of the 1,196 men on board survived the ordeal, which left the navy scratching its heads trying to figure out how this could have happened. When you have drunk, antisocial pranksters operating the controls, anything is possible.

TOO LITTLE, TOO LATE

In 2000, Congress exonerated *Indianapolis* captain Charles McVay, who had committed suicide thirty-two years earlier, of all responsibility for the attack. At least now he can rest in peace.

1948

WHEN CONVENTIONAL WISDOM DOESN'T HOLD TRUE

Dewey and Warren won a sweeping victory in the presidential election yesterday.

—Arthur Sears Henning, *Chicago Tribune*

The 1948 presidential election between Republican Thomas Dewey and Democrat Harry S. Truman was viewed by many pundits to be a done deal before voting even began. Then the American public took to the polls and turned those pundits into idiots.

Due to a writers strike, the *Chicago Tribune* had organized a more tedious newspaper printing process, which involved typing the copy, photographing it, then engraving it onto the printing plates. This resulted in the papers being printed hours earlier than they normally would have been. Knowing this, the paper decided to get a jump on printing their presidential edition. Political analyst Arthur Sears Henning, the Washington correspondent for the *Chicago Tribune*, assured the paper that the Republican nominee was in the driver's seat for the election, so the *Tribune* began to print early editions of the Dewey victory—even though early returns from the polls indicated a close race. You'd think that it would be better to get it right than to get it done early, especially for an important story like this, but Henning stuck to his conviction and the papers were printed with the banner headline "Dewey Defeats Truman" for its early edition. Later in the evening, with the race now well in doubt, the *Tribune* changed its headline to reflect the Democrat's victory, but it was too late for the 150,000 papers that were published. Truman won and the Democrats seized control of the House and Senate. The lesson? Even when you think you're right, it's probably best to make damn sure.

1949

———•—•———

AW NUTS!

That's a flying groundnut scheme, son.
—Spike Milligan, writer, *Private Eye*

Location, location, location. For any successful crop grower, this is at or near the top of the list of qualifications that you need to begin a job. If only John Wakefield had kept that in mind before embarking on his pea(nut)-brained trip to Tanzania.

Wakefield was in charge of finding a suitable area to grow peanuts to manufacture the oil needed for soap and margarine for Unilever. He decided to use this process as a teaching and learning tool for African farmers when he showed them how to take marginal land and resurrect it to bring about new crops. There was only one problem: The land Wakefield chose was much worse than marginal. The scrubland in the Central Highlands was a hideout for hundreds of bees, and the tree roots actually destroyed the machinery that was designed to take them out. To make matters worse, once they finally were able to plant the crops, they learned that the soil underneath (you know, where the nuts actually grow) was rock hard and made harvesting more of a chore than it was worth. When all was said and done, not a single nut was actually pulled to create the oil that was needed.

It would be one thing for a regular Joe off the street to commit this egregious of an error, but for a former director of agriculture? That explains the "former" in his title. What a nut job!

═══ ALLERGIC TO LOVE ═══

The Asthma and Allergy Foundation of America estimated that peanut allergies are the most common cause of food-related deaths (roughly 100 every year), and close to 3.3 million Americans are allergic to nuts. Guess they'll never experience the joy of a Reese's cup or a sticky PB and Fluff. Shame.

1954

ELVIS HAS LEFT THE BUILDING

You ain't going nowhere, son. You ought to go back to driving a truck.

—Jim Denny, manager of the Grand Ole Opry, to Elvis Presley

Elvis Presley is one of those celebrities who doesn't even need a last name. Just "Elvis" is fine. Everyone loves "the King" and loved him even when he was a rather rotund gentleman wearing a white, bedazzled jumpsuit.

But back in 1954, the world was just being introduced to Elvis's hot hips and rockabilly style. On October 2, Elvis performed at the Grand Ole Opry—America's bastion of country music. Not surprisingly, his performance (despite its many positive attributes) didn't go over well. The audience hadn't heard his type of music before, and their lukewarm applause politely told Elvis that they didn't care to hear it again.

Unfortunately, the Opry's manager, Jim Denny, wasn't so polite. After the show, Denny famously told Elvis, "You ain't going nowhere, son. You ought to go back to driving a truck." Elvis was not happy about the situation and swore that he'd never perform at the Opry again—which I'm sure the Opry regretted in 1956 when "Heartbreak Hotel" took the country by storm.

Elvis never did go back to driving that truck. But you wouldn't have known it to look at him when he died while sitting on his toilet in 1977—or did he?

FOR BETTER OR WORSE

In an odd plot twist, Elvis's daughter Lisa Marie married the King of Pop, Michael Jackson, in 1994. Their creepy kiss on the MTV Video Music Awards that year shocked just about everyone. But their love was not to be. They divorced twenty months later.

1955

◆━◆━◆

GO, SPEEDRACER, GO!

We need a signal system. Our cars go too fast.
—Pierre Levegh, driver who was killed in the accident

Pierre Levegh was a newly hired driver for a Mercedes that was participating in the big 24 Hours of Le Mans race on June 11, 1955. It's a job he probably should have passed up.

Levegh had encountered a pack of cars in front of him as he was making a turn, but traveling at 150 mph he had no chance to avoid the collision. When Levegh clipped the car in front of him, his car separated into several pieces and launched toward the crowd, where surely a barrier was built to protect the spectators from the debris, right? Yeah, not quite. The hood, engine, and burning fuel all found their way into the crowd, where there was no protection at all. Eighty-three fans and Levegh all died in the crash.

Pictures of the raceway show that the stands and race protection where the affected crowd was were basically the same as high school bleachers for football games—nothing higher than a chain link fence to separate them. Did the course officials all expect their drivers to be so perfect that there would be no crashes? These guys aren't exactly obeying speed limits here.

> **DO YOU FEEL LUCKY, PUNK?**
>
> A total of twenty-one drivers have died as a result of accidents at the Le Mans race track at an average of one every four years. With none since 1997, let's hope it stays that way!

1956

FULL STEAM AHEAD!

*I am sorry to have to inform you that we have collided with the Italian
ship the Andrea Doria.*

—PA announcement on the MS *Stockholm* after the collision

You'd be hard-pressed not to notice a 700-foot long boat on radar. But to not notice it in person as well? Tell that to the crew on board the MS *Stockholm*.

The *Andrea Doria* was en route from Genoa, Italy, to New York on the last night of its voyage across the Atlantic. On its way out of New York was the MS *Stockholm*, which was headed to Sweden. Little did the crew on the two ships know that they were on a collision course with each other. In an area that sees a lot of boat traffic, with heavy fog complicating matters, the *Andrea Doria* decreased its speed and activated all warning signals to alert other ships of its presence. Somehow the MS *Stockholm* missed these signals and the two boats proceeded to head toward each other, a disaster in the making. Each captain attempted to veer out of each other's way, only to steer in the same direction toward each other. Hello! Grab your radio and talk to each other! The MS *Stockholm* began turning to avoid a collision, but it was too late and the Swedish vessel struck the Italian ship at a 90-degree angle. The *Andrea Doria*—a ship deemed one of the safest ever built—sank in eleven hours. Looks like this ship was as safe as the *Titanic* was.

THE LITTLE BOOK OF BIG F*#K UPS 127

1959

━━◆◆◆━━

THE ULTIMATE LEMON

[The Edsel] was the wrong car at the wrong time.
—Jan Deutsch, Edsel scholar

Having worn out their welcome with the glut of Model T vehicles on the market decades earlier, Ford started using market trends to cater their new vehicles to the demands of the public. Which public they were catering to, however, is a big mystery.

Their new creation was called the Edsel, named after Henry Ford's son. Rolling the new vehicles out in 1957, in the midst of a recession at top-of-the-line prices, was a good way to get the public to bite. If the vehicle is good enough, maybe people will slap down the cash and take it home. Except the vehicle wasn't nearly as good as it was supposed to be.

Ford advertised the car as one with "more You ideas," but the ideas that "you" wanted were being constructed in the same shops as the other Ford vehicles. Picture Chevy makers being forced to make Ford cars. Why wouldn't they be all over it? Then, when the technology that "you" wanted made it into the cars, like the push-button gear changing, it was so advanced that mechanics couldn't fix it if something were to happen.

A poorly made car that's unfixable with features nobody wants that costs a lot of money . . . makes you wonder how it even lasted three years.

PLUG IT IN

While the Edsel was a tad ahead of its time with its technology, Ford has recently announced that they are working on an all-electric vehicle to be sold in 2011. Hopefully they'll get something right this time around.

1959

⊨⊷⊨

THE GREAT LEAP BACKWARD

I do not think that when he spoke . . . he knew how bad the disaster had become, and he believed the party was doing everything it could to manage the situation.

—Dr. Li Zhisui, Mao Zedong's personal physician

Mao Zedong, the Communist chairman of China at the time, seemed to have no bad intentions when initiating his grand scheme for China, which he dubbed the Great Leap Forward. If only he looked before he leapt, he may have had better results.

Zedong's plan was to completely transform the industrial nature of China in order to compete with the West by producing steel. Lots of steel. Farmers were ordered to produce steel—and nothing else—at the expense of their land. Lakes were filled in and rice fields were planted over, plus millions of people even built furnaces in their backyards to help fulfill the quota that Mao had set. Unfortunately, Mao failed to realize that his people were completely clueless about steel production. Rice farmers producing steel at the drop of a rivet? Townsfolk throwing their silverware into the furnaces to produce practically nothing worthwhile? While the results in the first two years were significant, remember those farms that were plowed over? The lakes that were filled in? Hey Mao, your citizens have to eat! A rice famine fell upon China and as many as 40 million people starved thanks to the Great Leap Forward. Mao forgot about the idea that if you starve your people they won't be around to use the steel that you've worked so hard to acquire.

1960

PATIENCE IS A VIRTUE

. . . program workers flouted safety rules in their haste to develop the first Soviet intercontinental ballistic missile, the R-16.

—AP article in *Pittsburgh Post-Gazette*, April 17, 1989

Like a child on Christmas morning, Marshal Mitrofan Nedelin was eagerly anticipating the "opening" of his gift—the launch of the first Soviet intercontinental ballistic missile on October 24, 1960. Little did he know that his impatience would blow up in his face.

The rocket was on the launch pad, ready to go, until they hit a snag. The fuel contained a type of nitric acid that was so corrosive that it could not sit in the fuel tanks for more than forty-eight hours without damaging the rocket. When the fuel accidentally leaked into the combustion chamber, the Soviets had to launch it the next day or wait several weeks to repair the engine. His patience tested, Nedelin ordered a next-day launch.

With time a wastin', Nedelin had his men move at warp speed to finish things up to get the launch in. Who needs safety skills when working with rocket fuel? Not coincidentally, a mix-up with the programming devices resulted in the second-stage engines firing up while the men were still around the rocket. The resulting flames ripped through the nitric acid tank in the first engine and blew up the missile. So much for an early launch. Nedelin and approximately 125 others died in the blast.

All they had to do was fix the first engine, test the components, and make sure all systems are a go for the big launch. That can't be that hard. I mean, it's not rocket science. Oh, wait . . .

1961

CAMELOT VERSUS CASTRO

Objective: The purpose of the program outlined herein is to bring about the replacement of the Castro regime with one more devoted to the true interests of the Cuban people and more acceptable to the United States in such a manner to avoid any appearance of U.S. intervention.

—U.S. Department of State's Program of Covert Action against the Castro Regime

In 1960, President Eisenhower decided it would be a good idea to train thousands of Cuban refugees to overthrow Cuban dictator Fidel Castro. The plan called for Cuban exiles to be trained in Guatemala and then return to Cuba to meet up with members of the underground anti-Castro movement to overthrow the government. What a great idea! At least that's what Eisenhower and his successor, President John F. Kennedy, thought anyway.

Kennedy had his doubts about the Bay of Pigs invasion, but by the time he got into office, he felt that the refugees' training had gone too far to back out. But there was a complete breakdown in communication somewhere along the line. He was told that the plan was unflappable, but in fact, the underground rebels in Cuba had no idea when the invasion was taking place—and it's hard to support an army if they show up unannounced.

In addition, due to the loose lips of some of the exiles and the U.S. media, Castro already knew that the invasion was forthcoming. So when the invasion took place, things didn't go well. More than 100 exiles were killed, the rest were taken prisoner, and the U.S. government was completely humiliated. The whole thing also didn't make Castro any happier with the United States, but it did make him a lot closer to his ally Russia and opened the door for the Cuban Missile Crisis in 1962. It's also the reason why you can't get a good Cuban cigar in the United States—and why Cubans have spent decades trying to make their 1956 Chevies seaworthy.

1962

◆━━◆

HOUSTON, WE HAVE A TYPO

[The Mariner 1] was wrecked by the most expensive hyphen in history.
—Sir Arthur C. Clarke, British author

The *Mariner 1* rocket was the first in a series of spacecrafts developed by NASA that would allow the United States to explore other planets. Little did they know how much a tiny little punctuation mark would cost them.

On July 22, 1962, NASA prepped their first spacecraft, the *Mariner 1*, for an exploration mission to Venus. Minutes after liftoff, the spacecraft veered off course, and NASA officials were clueless as to how it happened. No turn signal, no hand signal, nothing. Rather than risking the vehicle crashing into anything that would cause further damage, the decision was made to abort the mission.

What went wrong? NASA found two errors. The first was an issue with the radio guidance system, which was taken care of by having the guidance computer take over . . . which brings up the second error. The program in that guidance computer was missing a single hyphen. Not a paragraph of code, just one hyphen. This resulted in the spacecraft launching into a sequence of unexplained turns and maneuvers that threw it off course, resulting in the aborted mission. Total cost of that missing hyphen? Only $80 million. Fortunately a backup craft, *Mariner 2*, was ready weeks afterwards and completed the mission to Venus. They sure weren't going to forget the hyphen that time!

CHECK YOUR WORK

A New Mexico car dealership created 50,000 scratch tickets as a promotion with one ticket supposedly containing a $1,000 prize. Instead, a printer error resulted in all 50,000 tickets containing the $1,000 prize. In lieu of awarding $50 million to the ticket holders, they instead gave $5 Wal-Mart gift cards to each person. What a letdown!

WHILE MY GUITAR GENTLY WEEPS

We don't like their sound, and "guitar music" is on the way out.
—Dick Rowe, head of pop division, Decca Records

On January 1, 1962, Decca Records brought the Tremeloes and the Beatles in to audition for record contracts. They were searching for a new group that specialized in "beat" music. Decca would love to have a do-over of their fateful decision.

The Beatles arrived and performed a not-so-warmly-received set of fifteen songs. At the end of their set, the producers not so subtly said that "the Beatles have no future in show business." Decca opted to sign the Tremeloes, a four-man band led by Barry Poole, who were more local and would incur fewer travel costs for the record company.

After the rejection, the Beatles took their show to Parlophone Records, who wanted to meet the band after hearing their recording of the Decca audition (ironically enough). Not surprisingly, they were signed and began their historical career where they would prove to the world that they most definitely had a future in show business. What became of Barry Poole and the Tremeloes? It took several recordings for them to find success, but when they did, it was for cover versions of hits such as "Twist and Shout" and "Do You Love Me?" Advantage: The Beatles.

SIMPLY THE BEST

Pete Best was the Beatles' drummer at those Decca auditions but would only last another eight months with the band. John, Paul, and George parted ways with Best for reasons unbeknownst to him and hired Ringo Starr as the new drummer. Best can only wonder what might have been.

1963

An Italian Disastro

Millions of tons of earth and stone tore loose from Mount Toc and plunged into the Vaiont dam reservoir, 4 miles long and 440 yards wide. Displaced water flooded the lower Vaiont and Piave river valleys, destroying whole villages.

—*Chicago Tribune*, October 12, 1963

It's seen time and time again. Man ignores nature and does whatever the hell he wants with disastrous results. Which is exactly what happened in Italy in 1963 at the Vajont (or Vaiont) Dam, the tallest damn in the world (860 feet) at the time.

The Vajont Dam project was a f*#k up waiting to happen from the very beginning. The land the dam was built on was unstable, and the area had experienced frequent landslides for centuries. Sounds like a great place to cut into the earth, right? Of course! Once construction began in 1957, the earth around the dam started to shift and three different experts warned the Adriatic Energy Corporation, the dam's owners, that the landscape was likely to collapse. Did they listen? Of course not. Construction continued despite repeated warnings and a series of small landslides that threatened to overflow the dam. Instead of rethinking the project, Adriatic Energy pulled a dick move and sued the journalists who reported on the unsafe conditions.

In September 1963, it looked like the dam was about to collapse, and, instead of warning the people living in the villages below, the corporation tried to take matters into their own hands—and failed. On October 9, a major landslide overfilled the dam, and millions of gallons of water wiped out at least six or seven villages, killing up to 2,500 people. Looks like those engineers were right after all. Who would have thought?

1963

<hr/>

YOU DON'T ALWAYS GET WHAT YOU PAY FOR

It is virtually impossible to separate *Cleopatra* the movie from Cleopatra the spectacle—and that's because they are truly and rarely intertwined.

—From Contactmusic.com review of *Cleopatra*

The 1963 film *Cleopatra* won Academy Awards for cinematography, art direction, costume design, and visual effects. Little did 20th Century Fox know then how much those Oscars would cost them.

With a budget set at $2 million, the film was ready to go under director Rouben Mamoulian, until he was fired after he spent $7 million and had all of zero minutes of usable footage to show for his work. So much for a budget.

As if that issue wasn't bad enough, Elizabeth Taylor (who played Cleopatra) needed an emergency tracheotomy to save her life during the early stages of filming in London. Then, with the weather in England wreaking havoc on the exquisite sets and costumes, the team had to pack up for Rome to continue filming—and rebuild all of the sets again. More money out the window. What was 20th Century Fox paying for again?

Sensing that too much time had gone by without a f*#k up, Liz Taylor (Cleopatra) and Richard Burton (Mark Antony)—both married—began a relationship together that didn't go unnoticed by the press. The two would marry after filming (Burton would be husband number five of seven for Taylor, if you're keeping track).

When all was said and done, the film—with a $2 million budget—cost over $44 million (equal to roughly $307 million today) and ran for four hours and three minutes. The film was so long people couldn't even sleep through the whole thing! 20th Century Fox surely wishes they had slept on the offer to film it.

1964

THE HAPPIEST PLACE ON EARTH?

Whenever I go on a ride, I'm always thinking of what's wrong with the thing and how it can be improved.

—Walt Disney

Buckle Up. Fasten Your Seat Belts. No matter how it's worded, it's there for a reason. When one tempts fate by not following this order, the results can be messy.

Fifteen-year-old Mark Maples was out with his friends having a great time in Disneyland. Their next adventure would come on the Matterhorn roller coaster. They hopped in, buckled up, and enjoyed the climb up to the summit. Mark figured, somewhere along the way, that the ride itself wasn't fun enough. As the cars approached the summit, Mark unbuckled himself and stood up. Riders are scared s*#tless by being strapped in for dear life on these things, and here's Mark, standing up at the ride's highest point! Well, Evel Knievel he is not. Mark didn't get a chance to belt himself back in as he lost his balance and plummeted onto the tracks below. He would perish from his injuries four days later. Mark, that seatbelt wasn't there as a decoration!

> ## ═══ WATCH YOUR STEP! ═══
> The rides aren't the only attractions to be mindful of at Disneyland. Two overexuberant guests have died on the people movers, and one gatecrasher lost his life on the Monorail. Enter Disneyland at your own risk!

1967

WHAT'S THIS SCHLITZ IN MY BEER?

*That stuff was undrinkable in the '70s. It had a very
pronounced chemical taste.*

—John Gurda, Milwaukee historian and author

Schlitz beer—"the beer that made Milwaukee famous"—was the second-best
beer in America behind Budweiser in the 1960s and 1970s. In an effort to
surpass Budweiser, Schlitz made some bold moves that sent them up the list—
of America's worst beers.

In an effort to increase production while also trying to cut costs, Schlitz
introduced a new method of fermentation that accelerated the process and
swapped out their barley for a cheaper alternative—corn syrup. Schlitz even
resorted to building a new brewery designed for this new style. Making a good
beer takes time though, and you can't speed up time. The beer didn't stay fresh
for very long as a result, leading to an awful taste. Just as bad, the cheaper
ingredients adhered to form a filmy substance that lingered in the bottom of
the cans. That would be quite the surprise if you didn't know it was there, but
the brewery did know it was there so they decided to . . . do nothing. Were
they banking on the customers not noticing the creepy amalgam of goo in the
bottom of their can, not to mention the gross taste? If they were, they failed
miserably. Several months passed before they recalled any of the goo beers, and
in 1981 they shut down their Milwaukee plant. Schlitz turned into "the beer
that made Milwaukee infamous" with their less-than-stellar ideas.

1967

<hr/>

Can't See the *Forrestal* Through the Flames

The tragedy of the giant USS *Forrestal*, whose decks and men were seared and blasted by a series of explosions off Vietnam, was the second carrier fire in less than a year—the greatest calamity in carrier operations since WWII.

—The *New York Times*, August 1, 1967

The morning of July 29, 1967, a bunch of fighter planes onboard the USS *Forrestal*, a U.S. aircraft carrier stationed in the Gulf of Tonkin during the Vietnam War, were getting ready to take off when a Zuni rocket fired across the deck. It hit the fuel tank on a Douglas A-4 Skyhawk airplane, and that tank sprayed its fuel all over the deck, which was instantly engulfed in flames. The flames then caused other fuel tanks to explode and detonated nine bombs total, including an AN-M65, a 1,000-pound bomb. The explosions killed 131 sailors, injured another 161, and incurred $72 million in damages.

But why did the rocket accidentally fire? Turns out that each rocket has an electrical connector called a pigtail that transmits the electrical current that fires the rocket. Normally, the pigtail would only have been attached when the plane was in the catapult ready to launch, but the Weapons Coordination Board on board the *Forrestal* decided that, to save time, the pigtail could be connected while the planes were waiting in line to be launched. Guess that time-saving idea didn't really work out here.

Yes, war may be hell, but humongous mistakes made by the ones who are supposed to be in charge took this f*#k up to a whole other level.

> ## JOHN MCCAIN'S TOUR OF DUTY
>
> The Skyhawk airplane that was hit by the rocket was piloted by none other than 2008 presidential candidate John McCain. Not sure if the disaster on the USS *Forrestal* was worse than the one McCain inflicted upon himself when he chose Sarah Palin as his running mate.

1968

Do Not Adjust Your TV Sets . . .

I didn't get a chance to see [Heidi], but I heard it was great.

—Joe Namath, Jets quarterback

Have you ever noticed the huge gap of programming time between today's football games and the network's return to regularly scheduled programming? Well, it all goes back to a face-off between the New York Jets and sweet little milkmaid Heidi.

On November 17, 1968, NBC aired the Jets/Raiders NFL game at 4:00 P.M. and planned to immediately follow the game with a made-for-TV version of *Heidi* at 7:00. After all, what football fan wouldn't get excited about *Heidi*? As 7:00 P.M. approached, the Jets were ahead 32–29 and 1:05 remained on the clock. NBC tried to halt the switch until the game was over, but so many people were calling to see if the remainder of the game was going to be broadcast that the network couldn't get through to their own production trucks. With the exception of the West Coast, *Heidi* began right at 7:00 P.M. and all hell broke loose—both at NBC and in the football game.

In those final sixty-five seconds, the Raiders scored two touchdowns and came back and won the game, 43–32 . . . but nobody knew until a crawler appeared during *Heidi* to inform the viewing public. Football fans were outraged, and innocent little Heidi was reviled by millions of people all over the country. Today, football is buffered from the crap the networks show after football by an automatic time gap. Thanks for nothing, Heidi!

1972

Is It Over Yet?

Under FIBA rules, the United States won.

—Hans Tenschert, official scorekeeper for the 1972 gold medal game

A do-over in a playground basketball game doesn't usually lead to much commotion. Up the stakes and it will. In 1972, they were up as high as they could possibly get.

With three seconds remaining and the clock running, the U.S. men's basketball team led the Soviets 50–49 in the 1972 Olympic gold medal game. Confusion set in as to whether or not the Soviets had called timeout to stop the clock, so the officials reset the players to set up the last play again. The Soviets inbounded the ball and got off an obstructed three-quarters-length shot that missed by several feet as the horn sounded, signaling the end of the game—or did it? That horn went off before the clock—which somehow showed fifty seconds and not three—actually expired. Eh, three seconds, fifty seconds. No big deal, right? By this point, the crowd was on the floor celebrating a United States victory. Order was restored, the stunned crowd filed back in their seats, and the clock was reset yet again. For the Soviets, the third time was a charm. They completed the length-of-court inbounds pass for a layup and a gold medal. No resetting play this time around. To say the American squad was furious would be a humongous understatement. They refused to accept the silver medals and skipped the medal ceremony. Don't bother asking them for a do-over on that decision.

1972

TRICKY DICK

And in all of my years of public life, I have never obstructed justice. And I think, too, that I can say that in my years of public life, that I welcome this kind of examination because people have got to know whether or not their president is a crook. Well, I'm not a crook. I've earned everything I've got.

—President Richard Nixon

On June 17, 1972, five (obviously inept) burglars were caught breaking into the National Democratic Headquarters located in the Watergate Hotel in Washington, D.C. The bungling thieves were attempting to steal any info or secrets the Democrats had and wiretap the headquarters to help Republican President Richard Nixon win re-election against Democratic Senator George S. McGovern. Before all was said and done, it came out that the thieves had been paid by the Committee for the Re-election of the President (CREEP), and then all hell broke loose.

Taped telephone conversations between Tricky Dick and his aides surfaced and were subpoenaed by the Supreme Court. Why he was stupid enough to tape conversations revolving around his connections to the break in we'll never know. Nixon tried to keep the tapes from coming to light, but eventually he was forced to turn them over. The tapes were the nail in the coffin for pretty much anyone involved with the Nixon White House, including: G. Gordon Liddy, finance counsel to the Committee for the Re-election of the President; Dwight Chapin, Nixon's appointments secretary; L. Patrick Gray, acting director of the FBI; Richard Kleindienst, U.S. attorney general; H. R. Haldeman, chief of staff. Basically anyone and everyone involved with Nixon at this point was collateral damage, and Nixon himself resigned the presidency on August 8, 1974. And all because of some inept burglars and an Oval Office wire tap. God Bless America!

1973

◄═══◆◆◆═══►

MAY THE FORCE BE WITH YOU, MR. LUCAS

The Force can have a strong influence on the weak-minded.

—Obi-Wan Kenobi in *Star Wars Episode IV: A New Hope*

George Lucas is considered one of the most successful innovators in the history of film, thanks to the *Star Wars* and *Indiana Jones* franchises. History shows that he could also have a successful career as an agent.

In the process of creating *Star Wars*, Lucas was attempting to secure a studio for the film but kept getting turned down—until 20th Century Fox agreed to take on the Force. There was only one condition: Lucas had to waive his salary as the film's director in exchange for the licensing rights to the merchandise related to the film, all rights to future sequels, and 40 percent of the box office gross proceeds. Let's wait for the folks at Fox to stop banging their heads on their desks . . .

To make matters worse, those were the negotiations for just the first *Star Wars* film. Little did Fox know there would only be five more (remember, Lucas has the rights to the sequels)! In all, the six films generated $4.55 billion in box office revenue, and the merchandise generated another $10.6 billion. Lucas's salary trade for all those "worthless" contractual items ended up generating an eleven-figure sum in revenue. Talk about a solid return on an investment. When you have the Force, anything is possible.

══ HEFTY, HEFTY, HEFTY ══

In 1981, Columbia Pictures turned down *E.T.*, referring to it as a "wimpy Walt Disney movie." With *E.T.* raking in $792 million at the box office, Columbia looks like the wimpy one for passing on the film.

1974

TEN-CENT BEER NIGHT—NO, REALLY

I went with $2 in my pocket. You do the math.

—Tim Russert, former host of *Meet the Press* and spectator at the game

The Cleveland Indians were a dismal team in the midst of another dismal season and had dismal attendance records to show for it. Then someone came up with a brilliant—if not safe—way to fill those seats for the June 4 game against the Texas Rangers: Ten-Cent Beer Night! That's right. Eight-ounce cups of beer were only a dime. The fans were more than interested, and attendance for the game was more than triple their average for a home game. However, the further the game progressed and the more beer that was consumed, the more inebriated the crowd became. I know, like anyone could have predicted that?

In the ninth inning, the beer took over. A fan jumped on the field and tried to swipe the hat of Texas outfielder Jeff Burroughs. In the confusion, Burroughs fell. Thinking the fan attacked him, his teammates (led by manager Billy Martin, no angel himself) and even the Indians's players stormed the area with bats. Fans then joined in with anything they could grab—knives, rocks, bottles, even stadium seats. It pretty much looked like a scene straight out of *Gladiator*. Sensing disaster, the umpiring crew chief—who was struck with a chair in the fracas—gave Texas the victory via forfeit. It was about time *someone* had a good idea!

> ## SPEAKING OF GOOD IDEAS . . .
>
> As disastrous as the results were for this event, it was actually duplicated several times. The Milwaukee Brewers held one in 1976, but commotions in the stands led to a limit on purchases when they held it in 1977 and 1978. Additionally, teams in the Central Hockey League were banned from these promotions for five years after bench-clearing brawls resulted from an incident in the 1977–78 season.

1974

—➤·◆·—

FLIXBOROUGH'S CHEMICAL ROMANCE

During the late afternoon on 1 June 1974 a 20-inch bypass system ruptured
. . . which resulted in the escape of a large quantity of cyclohexane. The
cyclohexane formed a flammable mixture and subsequently found a source of
ignition. At about 16:53 hours there was a massive vapour cloud explosion
which caused extensive damage and started numerous fires on the site.

—Health and Safety Executive's Report of the Court of Inquiry

Everyone loves new neighbors. You make an apple pie, grab a cheap bottle of
wine (why drop money on the good stuff before you know if you like them?),
trot out the welcome wagon, and get to know each other. It's good times.
Unless your new neighbor is a huge chemical plant. Then you may want to
start house hunting, which is what the friendly folks in Flixborough wished
they had done.

The Flixborough Chemical Plant had had some problems from the start,
namely a leaking chemical reactor that they decided to bypass with some
temporary piping. Not a problem. There's nothing wrong with a temporary fix
at a chemical plant, right? Yeah, okay.

On June 1, 1974, the temporary bypass pipe ruptured causing toxic gas to
leak in to the air and then ignite. Twenty-eight factory workers were killed
instantly, and the explosion was heard up to thirty miles away. The town was
leveled, and it took ten days to put out the fires. And all because someone
decided to put a Band-Aid on a leaky chemical reactor.

There goes the neighborhood.

1974

You're Gonna Need a Bigger Boat

I couldn't possibly write Jaws today . . . not in good conscience anyway.
—Peter Benchley

You may be thinking that Peter Benchley's novel, *Jaws*, and Steven Spielberg's screen adaptation of the novel would be considered an unheralded success instead of an unmitigated disaster. After all, the book was on the bestseller list for forty-four weeks and the film grossed more than $470 million worldwide. However, due in large part to the shark phobia that *Jaws* inspired, some shark populations off the East Coast have seen their number decreased by up to 90 percent due to shark hunting.

After the film was released in 1975, men with low self-esteem who wanted to prove their manhood participated in shark-hunting tournaments in towns up and down the eastern seaboard. Maybe they wanted to get drunk and sing "Show Me the Way to Go Home." Maybe they thought killing a big fish would get them laid. Either way, they did more damage to sharks than a great white could possibly have caused to humans. Even *Jaws* author Peter Benchley, who passed away in 2004, said that he actually regretted writing the book in the first place. Benchley even became a shark activist and spent his life trying to remedy the damage he did by writing *Jaws* in the first place. Despite his regret, in 1991 Benchley wrote *Beast*, a book about a giant squid terrorizing Bermuda. Good thing no one knows how to find a giant squid—or they'd be in serious trouble, too.

DADA. DADA. DADADADADAD. DA DA!!!

Every year since 1987, the Discovery Channel has dedicated a week in July or August to sharks. According to Neilson Media Research, in 2010, Shark Week grabbed hold of more than 30.8 million viewers nationwide. Check it out at *http://dsc.discovery.com/tv/shark-week/*.

1975

⟫━◆━⟪

PUFFERFISH 1, KABUKI ACTOR 0

A single fugu contains enough poison to kill 30 adults and there is no known antidote.

—Steve Lohr, *New York Times* correspondent

Bando Mitsugoro VIII was a well-known Japanese actor who specialized in kabuki. A man of his stature was used to the star treatment that he received in his home country, but it was this star treatment that largely contributed to his untimely demise.

Mitsugoro was dining in a Kyoto restaurant when he placed an order for four fugu kimo fish, a type of pufferfish. This wasn't just your run-of-the-mill fish that you can order at your local deli and bring home for dinner. Fugu kimo fish (primarily the livers) are packed with a poison called tetrodotoxin, which is so potent that it only takes 1–2 mg to kill an adult human. Mitsugoro claimed he could withstand this poison, and with such a well-known personality requesting the fish, the highly trained chef couldn't turn him away. With a plate full of poison in front of him, Mitsugoro stepped up to the plate and ate the fish. It would be the last meal he ever ate, as just seven hours later, Mitsugoro was dead after he succumbed to the effects of the poisonous livers he had just consumed.

The poison Mitsugoro ate could have killed close to 100 humans ... and he thought he could withstand it all by himself? What the fugu was he thinking?

REVENGE OF THE FUGU

Naturally, fugu preparation takes an expert chef with years of training before he can be let into the real world and put people's lives at risk. Most of the fugu-related deaths nowadays are from fisherman who don't realize the danger of their catch when they eat it.

1976

BUY NOW, PAY LATER . . . OR NEVER

We gave credit to every deadbeat who breathed.

—Unidentified former manager of a W. T. Grant store (circa *BusinessWeek*, 1976)

The W. T. Grant chain of twenty-five-cent stores (named for its founder, William Thomas Grant) was a huge hit for over seventy years in the United States, but management made a critical error that led to the chain's sudden downfall.

Beginning in 1969, W. T. Grant extended credit to all of its customers. Due to the slow economy, the chain saw this as an attempt to bring more business into its stores and lure shoppers away from its rival store, Kmart. Unfortunately, when they meant "all customers," they meant *all* customers— regardless of their ability to repay the store. No background checks required. This went on for seven years, and nothing was done to change the policy. Compounding the issue was their ultrafast expansion in the United States— opening 369 stores in a five-year period—in smaller towns that couldn't sustain a huge chain location. Why didn't they just put the goods out in the street and let people take what they wanted? With goods going out and very little money coming in—with payment plans as low as $1/month, how could you not take advantage of this system?—they couldn't afford to restock and went belly-up in 1976. How ignorant did management have to be to not do anything about this? Maybe they were taking advantage of the credit plan, too? Mr. Grant would have rolled over in his grave if he knew this was going on.

1976

❖

A YARDBIRD FLYS THE COOP

Another veteran of the 1960s, singer Keith Relf of the Yardbirds, died last year with a guitar in his hand . . . So, kids, before you start thinking of getting into rock 'n' roll professionally, think of the toll it has taken on the music's biggest stars.

—The *Windsor Star*, December 10, 1977

In the 1960s, rock 'n' roll reigned supreme, and the lifestyle was pretty intense. Musicians dropped dead left and right from overdoses, heart attacks, overdoses, car/plane crashes, overdoses, and so on. However, you don't hear too much about rock 'n' roll gods who are killed by their own instruments, but that's exactly what happened to Keith Relf of the Yardbirds.

The Yardbirds were a British group famous for songs such as "For Your Love," "Heart Full of Soul," and " Over Under Sideways Down." And, when it came right down to it, Relf, who was the band's singer and resident harmonica player, really was the group's underdog; other band members included legendary guitarists Jimmy Page, who went on to form Led Zeppelin, and Eric Clapton. Working with these guitar superstars, you'd think he'd know a thing or two about how to handle the instrument, but that wasn't the case, and Relf was found dead in his damp basement on May 14, 1976, electrocuted by his own improperly grounded electric guitar. Everyone wants to die doing what they love, but maybe Relf should have stuck to the harmonica.

> ### IF AGE IS JUST A NUMBER . . .
> Then why do so many people die at age thirty-three? The death list includes John Belushi, Eva Perón, Chris Farley, Jesus, Eva Cassidy, and Cass Elliot of The Mamas & the Papas who, according to urban legend, died while eating a ham sandwich. So if you've made it to thirty-four, congratulations! If not, good luck!

1977

The "Lack of" Love Canal

Give me Liberty. I've Already Got Death.
—Sign on Love Canal resident's lawn

Residents in the Love Canal area of Niagara Falls, New York, had noticed a curiously high rate of cancer, birth defects, and pregnancy issues compared to those in other towns. Everyone was mystified as to what was causing this, but all it took was a few curious schoolchildren to figure it out.

While out on the playground at recess, the kids noticed an oozing black substance rising from the dirt. Black gold? Nope. Toxic waste? Oh yeah. Lots of it. Try over 20,000 tons of it, all underneath that school. The waste had been dumped there several years after World War II and was just now rising to the surface. The Hooker Chemical Company was responsible for the dump, and when they finished, they filled the contaminated area over with dirt and sold the land to the city for $1, where they began building their Love Canal community. Usually, items you buy for $1 constitute a good buy. In this case? I'm sure that dollar could have been spent better elsewhere.

Residents were strongly advised to not eat anything grown in their gardens and to be mindful of seepage into their basements. Yeah, that stench that's emanating from your basement? It's just toxic vapors. Don't worry about it. Commence mass exodus from Love Canal!

Families in the biohazard area were offered the opportunity to sell their houses to the government and hightail it out of there, and a large majority accepted. Over the next ten years, close to 90 percent of the Love Canal houses were abandoned. Where's the love?

1978

THE FALLING WALLENDA

Life is being on the wire; everything else is just waiting.
—Karl Wallenda

Karl Wallenda was the founding father (literally) of the Great Wallendas (later renamed The Flying Wallendas by the press), a circus group that became famous for their high-wire acts in 1928. Their first act was done without a safety net, as it was lost in transit, but they performed anyway to rave reviews. Performing without a safety net soon became their calling card. Talk about tempting fate!

Over the years, Karl lost four family members in high-wire-related accidents, but he didn't let those events keep him from walking the wire. At seventy-three years old, he signed on for a promotional walk between the two towers of the Condado Plaza Hotel in Puerto Rico. The towers were ten stories high, and Wallenda forewent the safety net, even at his advanced age. Hey, why stop now? While crossing, winds atop the towers reached 30 mph, and Wallenda fell to his death. While the thrill of the stunt is a sight to see, you'd think common sense would kick in at some point. Why tempt fate?

> ## ═══ WHAT A SLIP UP ═══
> While Karl died doing what he loved most, other daredevils weren't so lucky. Consider Bobby Leach, who successfully plunged over Niagara Falls in a steel barrel in 1911. Fifteen years later, he slipped on a deadly orange peel and died from complications of gangrene.

1979

Don't Have a Meltdown

The accident did *happen and potentially poisoning and lethal radiation* did *escape. Dangers do exist with nuclear power. Neither the machines nor the safety systems that surround them are perfect. If small mistakes can occur, large, very dangerous ones can also.*

—The *Milwaukee Journal*, March 31, 1979

On March 28, 1979, one of the worst nuclear events in U.S. history started to unfold. At the Three Mile Island Nuclear Generating Station plant in Pennsylvania, the pumps that moved water through the plant shut down, which kept the steam generators from removing the plant's heat. Obviously an overheated nuclear plant is bad thing, so the good news is that there was a relief valve that relieved some of the pressure. Unfortunately, the relief valve didn't close when the pressure went down, water poured out of the valve, and the nuclear reactor overheated. Why weren't the plant operators warned that there was a problem? They were. They just couldn't figure out what was wrong. Who did the United States put in charge of this thing anyway? Monkeys could have realized that something really bad was going down. But it wasn't until a second shift came in that everyone realized how much they had f*#ked up. By then it was too late and 32,000 gallons of radioactive material had already leaked out and contaminated the plant.

The cleanup of TMI-2 cost more than $975 million and took more than nine years to complete. However, it ended up being impossible to remove all of the radioactive material, and in 1988, the Nuclear Regulatory Commission decided that, while they *could* do more to clean up the mess, the levels of radioactive material were small enough that they weren't going to worry about it. Don't you just love a government that says, "Hey, we're okay with just good enough"?

1979

Shhh . . . President Carter's Hunting Wabbits

The President confessed to having had limited experience with enraged
rabbits. He was unable to reach a definite conclusion about its state of
mind. What was obvious, however, was that this large, wet animal, making
strange hissing noises and gnashing its teeth, was intent upon climbing into
the Presidential boat.

—Jody Powell, Jimmy Carter's press secretary

Who doesn't love a rabbit? They're cute. They're cuddly. They tried to kill
President Jimmy Carter . . . Yes, seriously.

In 1979, President Carter took a day off. (Yes, the U.S. Embassy in Iran
had been taken over and there were some serious fuel shortages in the country,
but Jimmy needed a personal day. Hey, at least he didn't take out a motorboat.)
Nothing like a nice fishing trip to alleviate stress. Unfortunately, that's not how
things ended up.

Instead of relaxing, Carter's boat was attacked by what the media called a
"killer rabbit." Carter's approval ratings were pretty dismal at the time, so it
was clear that the rabbit wasn't trying to get the president's autograph, but he
did get more than he bargained for. Carter desperately tried to get the rabbit
to swim off. He did very aggressive things, like splash water at it and try to hit
it with his oars. The rabbit finally took Carter's suggestion and swam away, but
the damage was done—for Carter. Not the rabbit. The press got hold of the
story and Carter was mocked relentlessly for not being able to defend himself
against a bunny. The incident was used to turn the public against Carter when
he ran for re-election in 1980. Ronald Reagan, who had never had a rabbit
incident, walked away with the election, and Carter was left with . . . well, a
pretty embarrassing f*#k up.

1979

THE WHO'S BOTTLENECK

(It looked like) if they opened too many doors, they thought they were going to get trampled or something.

—Ellen Betsch, concert attendee

Back in 1979, The Who was one of the biggest acts out there. Tickets sold out for their scheduled show at Cincinnati's Riverfront Stadium on December 3 in just ninety minutes. Most of these tickets were general admission seats, but when you have upwards of 14,000 people fighting for the best seats in the house, it can get a little crowded. And crowded is exactly how the stadium's main entrance looked when it came time to open the doors . . . or, more accurately, *door*. An hour before the start of the show, while The Who was conducting their sound check, an employee unlocked the one door he was responsible for and backed away. One door. For 14,000 excited people. People collapsed into the doorway as everyone did anything they could to get in. Articles of clothing were strewn about, and when the madness was over, eleven concertgoers were dead and dozens more were injured. That concert had better have been worth it! Riverfront Stadium, next time some forethought—and some door-opening courtesy—would be nice!

UPON FURTHER REVIEW . . .

Cincinnati promptly banned the use of festival seating at its concerts as a result of the tragedy at Riverfront Stadium, but when Bruce Springsteen was coming to town in 2004, they changed their minds. The fans were born to run . . . this time through all doors of the arena.

1979

DISCO INFERNO

*It was great until 10,000 people ran on the field and we
had to forfeit the game.*

—Mike Veeck, promoter

Sometimes even the best laid plans go up in smoke, which is exactly what
happened on the night of July 12, 1979, at Comiskey Park in Chicago.

Mike Veeck organized a Disco Demolition Night in conjunction with the
White Sox's doubleheader against the Tigers. Fans were encouraged to bring
their disco records to the park in exchange for an admission ticket. The records
would be collected at the gate and, in between games of the doubleheader,
blown up in center field. Close to 90,000 fans showed up in anticipation of the
event, and the staff couldn't fit all the records on the field. The ones that weren't
collected found their way on the field anyway, Frisbee style, along with beer
and firecrackers—during the game! Once the records were detonated (which
produced a hole in the outfield), thousands of fans poured onto the field,
lighting fires, stealing bases, ripping up the field, and causing a full-scale riot.
Did I mention that there was a second game to be played afterwards? Yeah,
that didn't happen. The Tigers were granted the win by forfeit. The promotion
was categorized (along with disco music) as a big giant clusterf*#k.

THE LAST HURRAH

Mike Veeck was the recipient of intense backlash surrounding the
event. The son of the White Sox owner, Bill Veeck, he was out of
baseball for ten years following this incident. There hasn't been an
American League game forfeited since then.

1980

MAN VERSUS THE VOLCANO

*If the mountain goes, I'm going with it. . . . the mountain
ain't gonna hurt me, boy.*

—Harry Truman, 1980

Harry Truman—no, not *that* Harry Truman—was a resident of Mt. St.
Helens, Washington, in the Mt. St. Helens lodge on Spirit Lake, right at the
base of the mountain. A nice, peaceful area to live—until that one day when
the mountain was more than just a good view from the lodge.

That one day—May 18, 1980—turned out to be the last for Mr. Truman. A
morning earthquake disturbed the molten rock and ash in the now-weakened
mountain, causing an eruption that shot 80,000 feet in the air and sent ash
flying into eleven states—as far as Oklahoma! All of a sudden, Mr. Truman's
lodge doesn't seem like the safest place to be. Given the seismic catastrophe
now upon him, you'd think it'd be a great time to high-tail it out of there,
right? Harry didn't think so, saying, "If it erupts with lava it's not going to get
me at Spirit Lake." It's one thing to be stubborn. It's another to be stubborn
and stupid. Snow, ice, mud, and just about anything else that was around the
mountain poured down into Spirit Lake and buried Harry's lodge with Harry
still inside. That mountain sure showed him a thing or two!

> ## THE BEST SEAT IN THE HOUSE
> Thirty-year-old volcanologist David Johnston was stationed at an
> observation post several miles from the volcano when he was killed
> from the lateral blast of the eruption. At least he had a good view!

1980

A *BLACKTHORN* IN THE SIDE

The Coast Guard buoy tender *Blackthorn*, a gaping gash in its port side, rose from the bottom of the Tampa Bay shipping channel Tuesday in a cradle of cable. Young Navy and Coast Guard salvagers set a new American flag to flapping on the ship.

—*St. Petersburg Times,* February 20, 1980

On January 28, 1980, the USCGC *Blackthorn* had just finished up a complete overhaul and was leaving Tampa Bay to head home. While the *Blackthorn* was on her way out of port, the Russian cruise ship *Kazakhstan* passed her on her starboard (right) side, leaving the *Blackthorn* in the middle of the channel. At the same time, the oil tanker *Capricorn* was trying to enter the port on the *Blackthorne's* port (left) side. Normally, the ships would be able to see each other's lights and would know how to proceed, but the *Kazakhstan's* lights blinded Ensign John Ryan, who had been commanded to steer the ship by Captain George James Sepel Jr., making it impossible for him to see the *Capricorn.*

Now, if you know anything about boating, you know that you can communicate with horn signals if you can't see another ship's lights. The *Capricorn's* captain blew his horn twice to let the *Blackthorn* know he'd pass on the starboard side, but Ryan didn't understand the message and the two ships collided; the *Blackthorn* capsized almost immediately, killing twenty-three of the fifty sailors on board. No word on why someone earning a living as a sailor didn't understand basic safety precautions, or why he was allowed to steer the ship through a busy channel. Bet Captain Sepel didn't make that mistake again.

1981

Don't Forget about Me!

I think I should have used more foresight about arranging my departure. I'll soon find out.

—Entry in Carl McCunn's journal

Wildlife photographer Carl McCunn was gearing up for his foray into the Alaskan wilderness. Film? Check. Food? Check. Ride there? Check. Ride home? Oops. In March 1981, McCunn organized a ride from a pilot to drop him into Alaska, where he would take pictures of the animals and scenery and would plan on staying until mid-August. It wasn't until shortly before he was supposed to leave Alaska that he realized his minor mishap in planning—how was he getting home? What's the point of taking all of those pictures if you don't get home to develop them and display them?

Sensing that he would be stranded, McCunn started hunting for additional food and even winterized his tent, just in case. He caught a break when his friends back home got concerned and sent the Alaskan police to check on their friend. They found him, but McCunn inadvertently signaled to them that he was okay, so they left without him. McCunn watched in agony as his potential last chance for getting home flew away. By November, having run out of food, McCunn couldn't take it anymore and ended his life with a self-inflicted gunshot wound. A sad end for a man that simply failed to ask himself one simple question: How am I getting home? Turns out he wasn't getting home at all.

OR ME!

In 1990, Christopher McCandless made his way to Alaska to live a life of solitude and died of starvation two years later. For his troubles, McCandless was the inspiration behind the film *Into the Wild*, which was also a novel written by Jon Krakauer. All Carl McCunn got for his journey was a mention in this book.

1982

Hershey's Goes the Extra Mile

Look what happened to Hermes scarves after *Basic Instinct*, Ray-Ban sunglasses after *Risky Business*, and suspenders after Michael Douglas wore them in *Wall Street*.

—Joel Henrie, partner, Motion Picture Placement

The world of advertising can be a ruthless bitch, and companies are constantly competing for prime ad spots. So, who would turn down a valuable marketing opportunity? Well, such was the stupidity of Mars, Inc. when they were asked about having their popular bite-sized candy, M&M's, showcased in *E.T.* For reasons that no one understands, Mars turned down the opportunity, which is too bad. Mars and aliens seem like a match made in outer space.

The folks at *E.T.* then went to Hershey's to ask for use of their Reese's Pieces, and Hershey's jumped at the opportunity. They actually paid to have their candy featured in the movie, and—as if that wasn't bad enough for the folks at Mars—Reese's Pieces were also used in the film's additional postrelease advertising. Sales for Reese's Pieces skyrocketed. Kind of like *E.T.*'s spaceship.

Maybe Mars thought *E.T.* was going to flop. Maybe they thought their resources were better used elsewhere. Or maybe they were afraid government agents would come after them in their homes. But either way, major f*#k up, Mars. And yes, Reese's Pieces are out of this world.

PAINFUL PRODUCT PLACEMENT

Not all product placement can generate the kind of boost that Hershey's got with *E.T. USA Today* was prominently featured in *Runaway Bride*, which did not do well at the box office, while the 1987 film *Leonard Part 6*—widely panned as one of the worst movies ever made—was viewed as a painfully long Coca-Cola commercial.

1982

A Championship Given Away

I hate to lose, but I can't let this affect my life.
—Fred Brown

The 1982 NCAA Division 1 championship basketball game between Georgetown and North Carolina featured firepower on both sides. Among the marquee names battling it out in the tournament were Patrick Ewing, Eric "Sleepy" Floyd, Michael Jordan, Sam Perkins, and James Worthy—who would find himself in the right place at the right time in the closing seconds of the game.

With Georgetown up 62–61, North Carolina swung the ball around to their hotshot freshman Michael Jordan, who gave the Tar Heels a 63–62 lead with just fifteen seconds to play. Then Georgetown's sophomore guard Fred Brown brought the ball up the floor, looking for an open man to set up the last shot. He picked up his dribble and spotted a teammate off to his right side out of the corner of his eye. Unfortunately, by the time Brown actually threw the ball, that teammate wasn't where Brown thought he was. In his place? Power forward James Worthy.

Now, Worthy was a great player, and there were plenty of people on the court who would have loved to have passed to him. The only problem is that all of those people were playing for North Carolina. Yes. Brown passed to someone on the other team—an athlete's worst nightmare. Worthy was fouled with two seconds remaining but missed both free throws. Georgetown then missed a last-second heave and North Carolina won the national championship—all with a little help from Fred Brown.

1983

DEATH BY EYE DROP

. . . deaths of this type are usually classified as accidental.
—Dr. Elliott Gross, medical examiner

Ah, Tennessee Williams. A depressing playwright who earned fame for winning two Pulitzers for his plays *A Streetcar Named Desire* ("Stellaaaaa!") and *Cat on a Hot Tin Roof.* Despite a fairly serious alcohol problem and a few bouts with depression, Williams was a pretty lucky guy. Unfortunately, his final act was as depressing—and disastrous—as some of his plays.

Williams was a playwright, which means that he likely spent a lot of time staring at his typewriter, anguishing about things like dialogue, rising action, and transformation. The staring at the typewriter, combined with the dry eye that probably came from a few too many Ramos Fizzes, eventually lead to Williams's death.

While applying eye drops, Williams had the bad habit of holding the cap between his teeth while he placed the eye drops in his eyes. Sounds tricky, right? Most people open their mouths when they mess with their eyes (ladies, you know you do it when you put on that mascara!). One night, while applying these eye drops, Williams's teeth lost their grip on the cap and it became lodged in his throat. Williams's secretary arrived the next morning to find him dead on the floor. Bad habits can be hard to break, but Tennessee Williams is proof that people should at least give it a try. Put those eye drop caps on the sink next time, okay!

> ## FOR YOUR EYES ONLY!
>
> In January 2009, a Missouri woman was arrested and charged with assault for trying to kill her husband by spiking his cup of tea with Visine eye drops. A similar event occurred in 2007 in a bar. Is any part of an eyedrop bottle safe?

1984

The Portland Trail Blazers Foul Out

There just wasn't a good center available. What can you do? Jordan isn't going to turn this franchise around. I wouldn't ask him to. He's a very good offensive player, but not an overpowering offensive player.

—Rod Thorn, then Bulls general manager, after selecting Jordan in the 1984 NBA draft

If you know anything at all about basketball, you know that this move was a huge foul. But what started the franchise on this long road to Loserville? Let's take a close look at the 1984 draft. All Portland had to do was make the pick that would solidify them as a contender in the West for years to come. Portland GM Stu Inman then narrowed his choice to two players:

- Sam Bowie with a stat line of 10.5 points, 9.2 rebounds, 1.9 blocks in his final college season—a season that came after he missed two entire seasons due to knee injuries. Can we say "red flag"?
- Michael Jordan with a stat line of 19.6 points, 5.3 rebounds, 1.6 steals, NCAA Player of the Year

Doesn't seem that hard, right?

Inman conferred with Bobby Knight, the then Indiana coach who had coached Jordan on the 1984 U.S. Olympic team. Knight tried to convince Inman to select Jordan, but Inman didn't listen (after all, what would a coach with two national titles and a gold medal know?) and fatefully selected Sam Bowie. Bowie would play in just 139 games over five injury-riddled (surprise!) seasons for Portland before being traded to New Jersey. Jordan, who was snagged by the Chicago Bulls, turned out to have a career that launched him into superstardom—and gave him a starring role in *Space Jam*, but that's a different topic all together.

1984

➤◆⟨

I Just Kept Running . . .

Keith Richards outlived Jim Fixx, the runner and health nut.
The plot thickens.

—Bill Hicks, comedian

Jim Fixx made a name for himself as an avid runner, releasing several books and becoming a cult hero amongst the running community. Fixx was living a somewhat unhealthy lifestyle when he decided to take up running. At 240 pounds and a two-pack-a-day smoker, he decided now was the time for a change. He lost sixty pounds and quit smoking over the next ten years, inspiring runners across the world. What was dangerous in Jim's case was that he had other health factors that should have been a red flag for him to take it easy.

Fixx had a congenitally enlarged heart, and his father died of a heart attack at forty-three. Fixx had already outlived his father to this point, but having also been a smoker in his earlier years, wouldn't this have been enough to want to slow down and not tempt fate? Fixx said no, and the irony gods would make their presence felt later on.

In 1984, after completing his daily run, Fixx—just like his dad—suffered a heart attack and died. He was only fifty-two. All three of his main arteries were at least 70 percent blocked as the aforementioned heart disease took him away. Fixx didn't learn from his dad's history and was doomed to repeat it. At least he died doing what he loved.

HOW DO YOU MEND A BROKEN HEART?

In 1963, Dr. James Corea, a well-known nutritionist and fitness expert, lived a similar lifestyle to Jim Fixx (postsmoking) and was seemingly a model of good health, but died at sixty-three from a heart attack. Heart disease is not to be messed with.

1984

ABC'S MISSED OPPORTUNITY

I don't see why they tried to hang this poor fellow over at ABC. He only was doing what they told him to do. Sitcoms are dead.

—Bill Cosby

Bill Cosby was contacted by Marcy Carsey and Tom Werner, former executives at ABC (remember that), about starting a sitcom. Cosby wanted the show to center around a financially stable African-American family with four children and to use the show to educate the viewing audience about a variety of important issues (such as teenage pregnancy and dyslexia) while playing around with his comedic background. With action-dramas such as *Dallas* and *Magnum, P.I.* taking over prime-time television in this era, a sitcom of this ilk would be a breath of fresh air to a newer audience.

Cosby and his team pitched the show to ABC—who said no. Lewis Erlicht, then president of ABC Entertainment, said that comedy on network television was "Dead. Forever." You don't say, Lewis, oh master of all things television? NBC, meanwhile, was lagging behind ABC and CBS in prime-time ratings and was more than willing to see what *The Cosby Show* was all about. The laugh was on ABC. *The Cosby Show* became the second show in history to top the Nielsen ratings for five straight years, and ABC's grip on the top spot in prime-time television was gone. I hope Bill sends Lewis a consolatory Cosby sweater.

THE RISE TO THE TOP

Following *The Cosby Show*'s reign, five other sitcoms would enjoy the top spot among the Nielsen ratings—*Roseanne, Cheers, Home Improvement, Seinfeld,* and *Friends*—while only *CSI: Crime Scene Investigation* has made it to the top among Lewis Erlicht's famed "action dramas."

1984

THE JOKE'S ON YOU, JON-ERIK

Let's see if I've got one for me.

—Jon-Erik Hexum, before his fatal accident

Jon-Erik Hexum, twenty-seven, was the male lead (Mac Harper) on the TV series *Cover Up*. Sequences were being shot for the season's seventh episode when there was a break in filming. There were more than just sequences that were being shot on set.

During downtime on set and in an attempt to be funny, Hexum grabbed a .44 Magnum and emptied all of the blank rounds except for one. Then he spun the barrel, pointed the gun to his temple and fired. So Russian roulette was his version of "funny?" No one on set thought it was funny. The impact of the blank dislodged a piece of his skull and propelled it into his brain, resulting in a massive hemorrhage. Hexum underwent emergency surgery to fix the wound but never recovered and was declared brain dead six days after the shooting.

Was there nothing else to do to pass the time on this set? A deck of cards? Mad Libs? Anything besides a .44 Magnum? At least play a game where there's a winner, because Russian roulette rarely has one.

FAMOUS LAST WORDS

Hexum's last words were quite eerie given the circumstances. Such was also the case for tenor Richard Versaille on January 5, 1986. While performing on stage in *The Makropulos Case* and standing on a twenty-foot ladder, he uttered the line: "Too bad you can only live so long." He then had a heart attack, fell off the ladder, and died.

1984

ROBBING PETER TO PAY PAUL

We regret having to conclude that, notwithstanding Mr Maxwell's
acknowledged abilities and energy, he is not in our opinion a person who can
be relied on to exercise proper stewardship of a publicly quoted company.

—Department of Trade and Industry (DTI) inquiry report on
Mr. Maxwell's companies

Robert Maxwell was a chief player in the worldwide publishing industry in the
1970s and 1980s, but how he got there led to a sad end.

Along with his publishing empire, Maxwell dabbled in politics and
promoted the Labour Party in Britain. As a man who also owned newspapers,
it practically made him free from criticism by the opposing parties—a criticism
he carried with him when he attempted to take over Pergamon Press from a
financial group, Leasco. When Leasco questioned Maxwell about Pergamon's
profits (how dare they!), he flipped out (which didn't help), which led to the
DTI investigation that revealed Maxwell's secret transactions between his
family companies. Sound practices for a "millionaire," aren't they? He made
a bad situation worse by continuing to buy publishing companies through
the 1980s and into the early 1990s by using pension fund money to keep
everything running. So that's where he got the money—he never had it!
Shortly after his last purchase, in November 1991, Maxwell's body was found
in the Atlantic Ocean after he had fallen from his yacht. His sons were forced
to file for bankruptcy the following year after falling hundreds of millions of
dollars in debt from their dad's work.

Maxwell was all talk in his claims to being this big, tough, rich guy when,
in reality, he wasn't that rich at all.

1985

The Train Wreck Everyone Saw Coming

I would say it is smoother, uh, uh, rounder, yet, uh, yet bolder . . . a more harmonious flavor.

—Roberto Goizueta, then CEO of Coca-Cola

Coca-Cola had dominated the beverage landscape for decades after World War II, when Pepsi-Cola entered the competition. By 1983, Pepsi had overtaken Coke in sales, thanks in part to younger soda drinkers that preferred the sweeter taste of Pepsi. Coke decided to make a drastic change to try to regain control of the soft drink landscape on April 23, 1985 . . . and boy, was it a mistake.

Instead of adding a new variety of Coke that could potentially dilute their sales, Coke decided to take their original product off the market completely and slap the "New!" Label on cans and bottles to emphasize the change. Did the executives fail to realize that, while trying to gain new drinkers from the revised formula, they could lose drinkers who wouldn't like it (the focus groups in their research strongly hinted at this)? The answer was a resounding yes. Hundreds of thousands of complaints poured into the corporate headquarters lamenting the loss of "Old" Coke. Even the bottling companies were concerned, stemming from a lawsuit over syrup pricing and the labeling of the product as "The Real Thing" when it had changed. New Coke lasted all of seventy-eight days before the switch was made back to the old formula. Coke, we hope you learned an important lesson here: If it ain't broke, don't fix it.

DON'T FORGET TO TAKE OUT THE TRASH!

It is the worst day in my life.
—Terry Yorath, Bradford City coach

The Bradford City soccer team had just wrapped up its most successful season in the club's history in 1985, winning the Division Three title and gaining a promotion to Division Two status. A celebration was planned for the day of the team's final game, May 11, 1985. Unfortunately for the city, the party went up in smoke—literally.

As the first half of the game wound down, smoke started emanating from underneath a row of seats, believed to be a result of a fan dropping a lit cigarette onto the grounds below. On the grounds was a pile of trash that had accumulated through the events at the stadium. That trash ignited and quickly reached the wooden stands. Within minutes, the fire spread all the way to the roof. Adding insult to injury, there wasn't a single fire extinguisher in the place due to a fear of vandalism. Chaos ensued all around the stadium as spectators crashed the gates to flee the engulfed stadium any way they could while the stands burned and the enflamed roof fell apart. Fifty-six people perished in the accident. Who said cigarettes were only dangerous when smoked?

BRADFORD'S BAD LUCK

Two years later, Bradford City caught another bad break, but this time it was on the field. They scooped prominent forward Gordon Watson on loan for £550,000—the most Bradford City ever paid for a player. Three games in, he was tackled viciously and broke his leg in two places. He would make only twenty-one appearances in three seasons with Bradford City before leaving the team.

1986

DUDE, MOVE ... MOVE! ... MOVE!!

Don't worry. We will pass clear of each other. We will take care of everything.

—Viktor Tkachenko, captain of the *Pyotr Vasev*, to the *Admiral Nakhimov*

In the southbound corner: *Admiral Nakhimov*, a Soviet passenger ship that contained 1,200 passengers and crew members en route to Sochi. In the northbound corner: the *Pyotr Vasev*, a freight ship en route from Canada. The two ships appeared to be headed straight for each other, so the captain of the *Admiral Nakhimov* (Vadim Markov) radioed a warning to *Pyotr Vasev* captain Viktor Tkachenko at 10:00 p.m. and was told everything would be okay. Except, it wasn't okay. Each ship kept chugging along as if the other wasn't on their horizon. Tkachenko never adjusted course as he intended (it's not like there was a humongous ship coming his ... oh wait). After several demands from Markov over the next hour, Tkachenko finally changed course—by 10 degrees. Way too little, way too late. Twelve minutes later, the *Pyotr Vasev* collided with the *Admiral Nakhimov* and tore a massive hole into the hull. The *Pyotr Vasev* received minimal damage, while the *Admiral Nakhimov* was no more—it sank in just seven minutes.

In the end, both captains were convicted of criminal negligence and served five years in prison. Strange how Markov tried so hard to get Tkachenko to move. Was Markov incapable of adjusting his own course? Turns out he was, based on court documents that showed Markov was absent from his post the whole time. Dude, move!

WHAT'S IN A NAME?

Two other ships named *Admiral Nakhimov* sank to the depths of the sea: a Russian armored cruiser in 1905 and a standard light cruiser in 1941. They always say the third time's a charm.

1986

See What Happens When You Don't Practice What You Preach?

I have sinned against you, my Lord.

—Jimmy Swaggart

In the 1980s, Jimmy Swaggart was one of the most successful televangelists in the world. If only he heeded the words of wisdom that he shared with his congregation, he wouldn't be the laughingstock that he is today.

In 1986, Swaggart exposed Marvin Gorman, a fellow minister based in Louisiana, for having a wandering eye when it came to women. Peeved about being exposed, Gorman called Swaggart out two years later for his extracurricular activities with a noted prostitute. Assuming Swaggart was not acquiring information to use in his next sermon, Gorman confronted him and made a deal where Swaggart would admit to lying about Gorman's prior affairs and Gorman wouldn't reveal what he just uncovered. Sounds fair. Who'd want to have their liaisons with a prostitute revealed to the public? Evidently Swaggart did, and soon his indiscretions were aired in grand fashion. He tearfully apologized in a speech that was considered so contrite that he was defrocked by the heads of his ministry group. It turned out to be a wise move as Swaggart would be caught with a prostitute again in 1991. Instead of confessing this time, he simply stated that "The Lord told me it's flat none of your business." Right. Just like the Lord told you to go "redeem" those ladies of the night?

PREACHER BY DAY . . .

According to a 2000 *Christianity Today* survey, 33 percent of clergy admitted to having visited a sexually explicit website. Of those who had visited a porn site, 18 percent visit sexually explicit sites between a couple of times a month and more than once a week. So much for practicing what you preach!

1986

BOB STANLEY KEEPS THE CURSE A COMING

Those fans who are booing me now will be cheering for me when I record the final out in the World Series.

—Bob Stanley, April 1986

Boston Red Sox first-baseman Bill Buckner gets all of the blame for blowing the most gut-wrenching baseball game in Boston sports history, but pitcher Bob Stanley really should take the credit for the BoSox's devastating loss.

All that stood between the Red Sox and baseball immortality in the 1986 World Series was a thirty-year-old slap hitter named Mookie Wilson. All Stanley had to do to win the game was record a third strike. Just one strike. Instead, he threw a wild pitch that allowed the tying run to score and the runner on first to advance to second. Wilson then hit a ground ball that sent all of Red Sox Nation into a collective depression that lasted for eighteen years.

Had the wild pitch not happened, Buckner would have been positioned at first base (holding the runner) instead of behind the base and off the line. Wilson's feeble ground ball would have come straight at Buckner, where he'd have a significantly better chance to field it cleanly, instead of making him move on his balky ankles and, well, allowing the ball to go where it went. Even if Buckner didn't field it cleanly, the game would be tied, and who knows how it would have ended.

Just one strike, Bob. That's all you needed. Was it really so much to ask for? Curse you and your little Bambino, too!

1988

Don't Drink the Water in Camelford!

The acidity of the water caused by the aluminum sulphate stripped a cocktail of chemicals from the pipe networks as well as lead and copper piping in people's homes.

—Irwin Mitchell LLP

On July 6, 1988, a delivery of aluminum sulfate was in process for the Lowermoor Water Treatment Works, the company that treated the water before it reached the town of Camelford, Cornwall, England. A relief driver was on hand to make the unsupervised delivery and was given a key for the tank—except the key opened just about every single lock and manhole cover in the facility. Not knowing this, the driver deposited the aluminum sulfate into the tank he incorrectly assumed to be the correct one, contaminating clean water with as much as 3,000 times the admissible concentration of aluminum.

Almost immediately, the South West Water Authority (SWWA) started receiving calls regarding the water's condition. They told residents to just mix it with orange juice to cover up the taste. Wrong answer. It took nearly a week to identify the cause of the poisoning, and even then the ignorance continued. On two separate occasions, government-appointed advisory groups found no evidence of aluminum poisoning and deemed the suffering as being provoked by anxiety. No apology. No convictions. No common sense applied. Let's save some of that water for them—but don't forget to cover up the funny taste with orange juice!

> ### STOP POISONING US!
> This wasn't the first time England had to deal with a mass contamination problem. Close to 1,000 houses in the Armley area of Leeds were contaminated with asbestos dust from the nearby factory that closed in 1959. The Leeds city council did nothing to inform the public as the number of mesothelioma deaths climbed. Sound familiar?

1989

CHARLIE HUSTLE'S HUSTLING PROBLEM

I bet on my team to win every night because I loved my team,
I believed in my team.

—Pete Rose, in an interview with ESPN's Dan Patrick in 2007

Pete Rose played in more games than any other major league baseball player, but it was his actions as a manager that had him embroiled in a controversy never seen before in baseball's history.

Before the 1989 season, Rose was questioned by MLB commissioner Bart Giamatti on his alleged gambling on baseball games, which he denied. The following month, evidence was introduced that showed Rose had indeed placed bets on games where he bet in favor of the Cincinnati Reds—the team he managed. Again, Rose denied the claims. These reports weren't just for one game here, one game there. Fifty-two games were described in these reports. After bickering with the commissioner for several months, Rose accepted a permanent placement on the ineligible list for the Hall of Fame in exchange for MLB dropping their investigation into his gambling charges. Um, Pete? They already found stuff on you. You whiffed on that deal. Rose could apply for reinstatement in one year, but unfortunately for Rose, Giamatti died just eight days after the agreement. Rose never got the chance to apply under commissioners Fay Vincent and Bud Selig and remains banned from the Hall.

As for gambling on baseball? Rose finally did admit to that—fifteen years later while in the midst of a book signing tour. How convenient! Looks like Fay and Bud have been doing the right thing all along.

1989

AUTOPILOT, MY ASS

Researchers expected the oil to break up in a few years. Instead,
it will take more than a century.

—*Wired Science*, March 24, 2009

On March 23, 1989, the soon-to-be-loathed *Exxon Valdez* left the Valdex oil
terminal en route to California with fifty-five million gallons of oil in its tanks.
After a little maneuvering around icebergs (read: the ship was sailing in the
wrong shipping lane), the ship's captain, Joseph Jeffrey Hazelwood, left Third
Mate Gregory Cousins and Able Seamen Robert Kagan in charge and went
downstairs to take a nap (some say he spent too much time at the ice luge the
night before, but that's never been proven). The ship was on autopilot, so what
could possibly go wrong? Absolutely everything.

Neither Cousins nor Kagan had gotten their required rest the night before
and legally weren't even supposed to be working that night. In addition, the
ship's radar had been broken for almost a year, but the equipment was deemed
too expensive to fix. (Hey, what ship needs something like radar anyway?) Due
to the lack of sleep and the fact that he had no idea where he was or what he
was doing, Cousins effectively rammed the ship into Bligh Reef just an hour
after his boss had left him in charge.

Oil poured into Prince William Sound to the tune of somewhere between
eleven to twenty-five million gallons and eventually covered 11,000 square
miles of ocean. The area was so isolated that reaction time was slow, and when
all was said and done, close to 250,000 birds, 2,800 sea otters, 300 harbor seals,
247 bald eagles, and 22 killer whales were dead. The oil was never entirely
cleaned up, and animal populations are still being affected—and all because
one man needed a nap. Next time, grab a Red Bull, a Garmin, and a quick nap
before you leave port. Asshole.

1989

THE HERSCHEL WALKER TRADE

That's why at the press conference I said "This is a great train robbery."
Everybody looked at me like I was a complete fool, including Jerry [Jones],
because they weren't sure we could pull this thing off.

—Jimmy Johnson, former coach, Dallas Cowboys

Herschel Walker was an all-everything running back entering his fourth NFL season with the Dallas Cowboys in 1989. Coming off of a 3–13 season in 1988 and already 0–4 to start 1989, the Cowboys brain trust wanted to get better in a hurry. Walker was the only All-Pro player on their roster and, on a bad team, clearly the only player of worth. Trade or not to trade, that was the question. Dallas decided to trade and got the Minnesota Vikings to bite on a last-minute deal. Thinking they were just one star running back away from the Super Bowl, the Vikings threw caution to the wind and traded five players and eight draft picks to the Cowboys in exchange for Walker and four draft picks. Turned out to be not such a great idea.

The Cowboys parlayed those draft picks into several trades that allowed them to draft Emmitt Smith, Darren Woodson, Russell Maryland, and Alvin Harper, setting the foundation for a Super Bowl wins in 1992, 1993, and 1995. Meanwhile, Walker played a whopping forty-two games over three seasons in Minnesota, who failed to reach the playoffs each season. Minnesota had to wait another six seasons before they would win a playoff game, and they still haven't made it to the Super Bowl. Maybe they're still just one running back away . . .

1990

BLAME IT ON MILLI VANILLI

We wanted to give the Grammy back. We felt in our hearts that it would be a good gesture to do that. But they made it look as though (the academy) wanted it back. They could have come to my house and gotten it.

—Fab Morvan

In 1989, Fab Morvan and Rob Pilatus of Milli Vanilla were flying high. Their album *Girl You Know It's True* had gone six times platinum, they were selling out venues around the world, and they had won the Best New Artist Grammy in early 1990. Too bad neither Fab nor Rob actually sang a word on stage or on their album. Instead, the vocals were performed by a group of unattractive, unmarketable singers named Charles Shaw, Brad Howell, John Davis, and Jodie and Linda Rocco.

Things started to unravel during a live MTV performance in late 1989 when the tape Rob and Fab were lip-synching to skipped. They tried to keep it together but ended up running off the stage in embarrassment. Then Charles Shaw told the media that he was the voice behind Milli Vanilli—guess he wanted in on the whole fame thing when he saw all the fun Rob and Fab were having—and Milli Vanilli's founder, Frank Farian, admitted to the media that Rob and Fab were fakes.

Turns out that people didn't like being duped. Milli Vanilli's Grammy was rescinded, and Arista records dropped the act from their label and deleted the album from their catalog. Fans got in on the action too and won a lawsuit that allowed close to 10 million buyers to receive a refund for any Milli Vanilli merchandise. Looks like Rob and Fav should have put some of that blame on themselves after all.

1991

<hr/>

Don't Let the Door Hit You on the Way Out

It seemed like the logical progression for home game systems. Nintendo certainly didn't want to be left behind when the predicted multimedia revolution began.

—HuguesJohnson.com

The idea behind the PlayStation console was a joint collaboration between Sony and Nintendo that came to fruition at a trade show in 1991. The console, called the Super Nintendo Entertainment System (SNES), contained a built-in CD-ROM drive as well. Cutting-edge gaming technology was upon us. Then, just as quickly, Nintendo backed out of their partnership with Sony in order to join with Phillips and compete with Sony on the gaming front. Nothing like a little friendly competition to spice things up, right?

Sony had a head start on the use of the CD-ROM attachment for their gaming systems, and their first consoles were compatible with both SNES games as well as CD games and audio CDs. Nintendo, meanwhile, was getting nowhere with developing a use for a CD-ROM attachment for it's clunky-looking systems. It was bad enough that we had to blow on those cartridges until our faces turned blue. What would Nintendo have us do with CDs? Thankfully, we'd never find out.

Sony would later remove the SNES gaming ability from its system, and their new design—a CD-only system—was called the PlayStation. This system became the first gaming system to sell over 100 million units. Nintendo never had a chance. So much for Mario and Luigi's dream of being on CD.

1991

TIME TO OVERTHROW SADDAM . . . OR . . . NOT

Trying to eliminate Saddam . . . would have incurred incalculable human and political costs. . . . We would have been forced to occupy Baghdad and, in effect, rule Iraq.

—George H. W. Bush, from *A World Transformed*

President George H. W. Bush launched a military offensive against Iraq that was considered to be largely successful, except for one minor detail. If only there was an alternate ending . . .

Saddam Hussein had ruled Iraq with an iron fist, and he wasn't afraid to use it. His militant tendencies toward those in his own country and in neighboring Kuwait prompted the United States to take action in what became the Persian Gulf War. With the Iraqi forces failing to surrender, the United States stepped up their game and got their wish. Now all Bush had to do was remove Hussein from power and the Iraqis could finally live in peace. Instead, Bush stopped. Not wanting to risk the lives of more American soldiers, he decided not to continue with the offensive. Not cool, man. Not cool. Why stop there? Why keep Hussein in power when he was the one in charge of the ruthless acts that got our country involved in the first place? Finish what you started, don't just quit while you're ahead.

═══ NOT AGAIN! ═══

Twelve years later Bush's son, President George W. Bush, would launch an attack on Iraq, which was still under the control of one Saddam Hussein. Of course, this could have been prevented had the elder Bush done his job in the first place.

1991

The Only "Chickens" Here Were the Owners

The Reagan and Bush Administrations I think have generally favored state plans and they have been approving them essentially regardless of whether or not they meet standards.

—Margaret Seminario, director of health and safety, AFL-CIO

Building inspections, while obnoxious, are done for a reason. And when factory owners don't get their buildings inspected, the consequences can be dire.

Such was the case on September 3, 1991, at the Hamlet chicken processing plant. The day started like any other, until one of the deep-fat fryers exploded. It didn't take long for the fire to spread and for people to realize that all of the fire doors were locked. The majority of the workers made it out without injury, but what were the factory owners thinking? Did they think someone was going to walk away with their raw chickens? It was later found that the owners had never had a safety inspection done in the building's eleven years of operation. Not one walk-through. Ever. What did they think was going to happen?

Several new intense safety regulations were put in place as a result of this fire, but it came as a result of a devastating incident like this. Too bad the owners didn't have a simple building inspection—something that could have saved them the trouble of spending the next twenty years in prison.

CHECK IT OUT!

The lack of inspections weren't solely restricted to the Hamlet plant. In 1977, the Beverly Hills Supper Club saw a major fire that claimed the lives of 165 people as a result of faulty wiring. The governor called it an "electrician's nightmare." Just call an inspector next time. It's much cheaper.

1991

WHEN RATNER SPOKE TOO SOON

I kept thinking that it would soon be over and that people would forget about the speech, that they'd stop calling me Mr. Crapner, and that the phrase "doing a Ratner" would disappear.

—Gerald Ratner, former CEO of Ratners jewelry stores

Have you ever had one of those moments where you said something and soon afterwards you realized, "You know, I probably shouldn't have said that"? Gerald Ratner knows that feeling all too well.

Ratner started in the family's jewelry business at age seventeen and built a highly successful chain of Ratners jewelry stores. The products Ratner sold were affordable but tacky and gaudy. Not that the public cared. Jewelry for low prices? Done!

In 1991, Ratner was at a convention in London when he was asked how he could sell these items in his stores for such a low price. Intending to be funny, he responded, "Because it's total crap." Oh boy.

The public noticed and, not appreciating the fact that they were buying crap, decided not to buy crap anymore—even returning crap that they had purchased prespeech. Ratner issued a public apology, but it was too late. His company lost £500 million (approximately $855 million), and he was removed from his position as CEO. So much for getting the last laugh.

THE FAMILY JEWELS

In the Victorian era, people who lost loved ones would commission jewelry made from the hair of their dearly departed. We've progressed as a society quite a bit since that time, and today companies such as LifeGem (*www.lifegem.com*) allow us to turn our dead relatives into diamond jewelry. Crap? No. Creepy? Without a doubt.

1992

EVEN PRESIDENTS NEED SICK DAYS

I'm very fortunate that in all the years that I've been President, I don't think I've had much of [the flu].

—George H. W. Bush, at a news conference on January 9, 1992

On January 8, 1992, President George H. W. Bush was in Japan meeting with Prime Minister Kiichi Miyazawa and enjoying a formal dinner, partaking of the local cuisine. President Bush indicated he wasn't 100 percent healthy earlier in the day, feeling the effects of the flu, but opted to go ahead with the dinner anyway. It's not like you can reschedule a trip to Japan. In the middle of the meal, Bush began to wobble and slumped over into Miyazawa's lap, completely passing out. (Too much sake perhaps?) First Lady Barbara Bush picked him back up, grabbed her napkin, and held it at his mouth. One napkin wasn't enough as Bush vomited off the napkin and right onto Miyazawa's lap. The Secret Service then jumped in to assist the president, who was back on his feet in a few minutes, where he would apologize to Miyazawa and the congregation before turning in for the evening. If he didn't like the food, why didn't he just say so beforehand instead of dumping it back on the prime minister's lap? At least he could have saved himself the trouble by staying in.

═══ RELAX! I'M OKAY! ═══

As if this incident wasn't bad enough, Bush had to quell rumors from the press afterwards that he was going to step down as president due to his health. Bush maintained he was okay, but the same couldn't be said about Miyazawa's suit.

1992

―――⟫•⟪―――

Brett Favre's Worn-Out Welcome Mat

I had to get him out of Atlanta . . . I could not sober him up.
—Jerry Glanville, former coach, Atlanta Falcons

In 1991, Brett Favre was a rookie quarterback for the Atlanta Falcons looking to make a good impression. But it didn't seem that he was trying that hard; Coach Jerry Glanville didn't approve of Favre's lifestyle off the field. Favre would frequently show up late for meetings and wouldn't always stay awake when he did show up. (Hey, he was only making a few million dollars. Why bother to put in the effort?) Glanville let Atlanta's general manager (GM), Ken Herock, know how little he thought of Favre and essentially forced the Falcons to trade for another backup quarterback.

With Favre now entrenched as the third-string QB, Herock received a call from Ron Wolf, then GM of the Green Bay Packers. Wolf was with the Jets in 1991 and had intended to draft Favre one pick after the Falcons selected him. Now with the Packers, Wolf put the pressure on Herock to make a deal. Herock didn't want to give up on his young QB but caved in to pressure, receiving a first-round pick from the Packers in exchange for Favre. That pick was used to select running back Tony Smith, who only played three seasons—well under the number of seasons Favre spent playing his "Will I retire?" game. Favre started every game since Sept. 27, 1992, until that streak finally ended when Favre was knocked out of a game on Dec. 5, 2010, and couldn't start the team's next game the following week. Too bad he wasn't starting for the Falcons.

HE'S BAAAACK!

Ron Wolf came full circle with Favre when he rejoined the New York Jets and traded for Favre for the 2008 season, but the Jets lost four of their last five games and missed the playoffs in Favre's only season with the team.

1992

DAN QUAYLE: SPELLING CHUMP

. . . it seemed like a perfect illustration of what people thought about me anyway.

—Dan Quayle

It was an exciting day for the youngsters at Munoz-Rivera Elementary School in Trenton, New Jersey, on June 15, 1992. Vice President Dan Quayle was visiting on his campaign tour to direct a mock spelling bee. But by the end of the day, the spelling bee wasn't the only thing that was mocked.

With a few words under his belt, Quayle selected William Figueroa as the next speller, asking the boy to spell "potato." William did this, but Quayle indicated via his flash card that "potato" should be spelled "potatoe." A confused William sat back down, but a reporter took notice of the error and pointed it out. Shortly after, the whole country found out what kind of a speller Mr. Quayle (spelled correctly, with an e on the end) was.

The public's perception of Quayle was already sketchy, and this certainly didn't do anything to dissuade that opinion. Five months later, the voters spoke—and it wasn't for Bush-Quayle. Bill Clinton became the new president with Al Gore as his VP. Wonder if Quayle knows how to spell "loser"?

VICE PRESIDENT OF F*#K UPS

Dan Quayle has recent company when it comes to VP screw ups. His successor, Al Gore, claimed to have invented the Internet, while Gore's successor, Dick Cheney, shot his friend, Harry Whittington, in the head and torso on a hunting trip in Texas. What could Joe Biden be up to?

1993

—◆◆◆—

HURRY UP AND FINISH, EVEN IF IT'S WRONG!

The inexperienced crew did not realize the hazards inherent in this dangerous practice and were being pressured to finish these scenes on time and under budget.

—Dave Brown, firearms safety specialist

Of all the props in a film to be modified unbeknownst to the rest of the crew, a gun should not be on that list. Brandon Lee found out the hard way.

While filming *The Crow*, Lee's character was supposed to be shot as he walked into a violent scene. The crew was behind in filming, so to imitate real bullets, they made "dummy cartridges," where the propellant and primer (the item that ignites the gunpowder) would be removed so that upon firing nothing would eject from the gun. Sounds simple enough . . . except the primer was still in the dummy cartridges. Even with no gunpowder, the primer can be enough to propel the bullet from the gun. What kind of crew is this? Forgetting to take out a piece of the bullets to keep them from firing at people? This is a real gun! Who cares if you're behind schedule? Safety first!

No one noticed the error, and the blank cartridges were placed in the gun. Lee entered the scene and expected to be shot with the dummy cartridge but got shot with a real one instead. The crew acted quickly to get medical help, but Lee passed away that afternoon.

All it would have taken was a second set of eyes to check the cartridges before they were used. You know, to make sure no one actually gets shot.

1993

UNC Has It Handed to Them . . . Again

It's a shame that Michigan will probably get some new label for losing this game.
They came this close to winning two titles and being labeled a dynasty.

—Pat Sullivan, UNC forward

We've seen some bad luck in the NCAA men's basketball title game (go back to 1982 and take a look at Fred Brown's doozy), and it seems that the University of North Carolina is always involved. In 1993, UNC's opponent was the University of Michigan, a team with a starting lineup composed primarily of underclassmen known in basketball circles as the Fab Five, led by sophomores Chris Webber and Juwan Howard. With the game already in overtime and UNC holding a 73–71 lead, Webber rebounded a missed free throw with nineteen seconds remaining. He raced up the floor and called for a timeout to try to set up a final play. A sound decision for a young team . . . when there's a timeout left to use. Unfortunately, that wasn't the case here. Seems like Webber had some kind of a brain fart, because the coaching staff reminded the players just minutes earlier during their *actual* last timeout! A technical foul was assessed, and UNC hit the ensuing free throws to wrap up the win.

Poor Michigan. All the hard work, all the preparation, all the grinding through tough competition to be at the cusp of dominance, only to have Chris Webber throw it all away as quickly as you can say "timeout."

ALL FOR NAUGHT

Even if Michigan had won the title, it would have been taken away. In 2002, an investigation found that several Michigan players were paid large sums of money by a booster. One of those players was Webber, who reportedly received over $200,000. All wins in 1992–93 along with their tournament appearance were vacated.

1995

NOT GUILTY? COME AGAIN?

If [the glove] does not fit, you must acquit!
—Johnnie Cochran, attorney for O. J. Simpson

October 3, 1995, was judgment day for O. J. Simpson. His murder trial complete, all that was left was the verdict, and it was . . . not guilty? Even O. J. couldn't believe it.

Every single piece of DNA evidence pointed to O. J. Simpson. From the blood on the gloves, the blood in the white Bronco, blood on O. J.'s socks—you get the idea. Solid evidence in any case, but the defense team showed that the prosecution mangled the evidence just enough to cast doubt in the jurors that it was legit. Granted, DNA evidence was relatively new to court cases in the mid-1990s, but the odds of that blood not being O. J.'s were about 172 million to one. And the prosecution still couldn't convince the jury?

Then there was Mark Fuhrman, the LAPD detective who discovered a majority of the evidence at the crime scene. Fuhrman's credibility was shot down by the defense when he lied on the stand about being racist. He's going to do that just three years after the L.A. riots resulting from the Rodney King beating? Nice timing. So much for his testimony.

But the greatest failure on the prosecution's part was the decision to try on the bloody gloves. They had no idea whether or not they would fit, and O. J. had to wear latex gloves when trying them on. Of course they wouldn't fit! The prosecution placed blame on the blood testing that resulted in shrinkage. Sure. Don't pull a muscle while reaching for excuses.

The LAPD turned this case from a walk in the park to a comedy of errors, and America had to sit back and watch as O. J. went on his search for "the real killers."

1995

It Was Divine

*I think you know in life what's a good thing to do and what's a bad thing,
and I did a bad thing. And there you have it.*

—Hugh Grant

Hugh Grant had it all going for him in June 1995. His first major film, *Nine Months,* was set to be released in theaters in just a few weeks. He was dating a beautiful British model and actress, Elizabeth Hurley. Then, for some reason he decided to listen to something other than his brain—and that head told him to do what even he admitted was a very "bad thing."

On the evening of June 27, Los Angeles police arrested Grant on a count of misdemeanor lewd conduct for his "actions" with a prostitute named Divine Brown. He was caught in his car with his pants down—literally. The police grew suspicious of Grant's parked car because the brake lights kept turning on and off; I'll leave it up to you to figure out why. But here's a hint, he wasn't hitting the brakes to call off whatever it was Divine was doing. The whole thing was made even worse because for $100 Brown would have taken Grant to a private hotel room, but Grant said he only had $60 in his pocket. See what happens when you don't carry cash?

As an added irony, Brown managed to work her magic on the media and turned that $60 trick into roughly $1.6 million from interviews, ads, media appearances, and so on. Guess the world was curious to find out more about the woman that Grant would cheat on Elizabeth Hurley for! FYI: Hurley dumped him soon after.

1995

You Can't Beat the Original

I still think it's the best idea I ever had, and the worst executed.
—David Novak, chairman, Yum! Brands, 2007

Crystal Pepsi's marketing slogan was "You've never seen a taste like this." The public would quickly realize that they didn't want to see a drink like that, let alone taste it.

In 1992, the advertising trend du jour was to invoke purity and cleanliness. Hey, it worked for Ivory soap! PepsiCo jumped on board the bandwagon and tried to turn Pepsi into a clear, clean version of itself. Were they trying to fool people? Hey look, it's Crystal Pepsi! Still tastes like regular Pepsi, but it's clear! This marketing scheme is right up there with the "alternate" home jerseys that your favorite sports team tries to shove down your throat. It's just another trinket in the stores that puts a couple of extra bucks in the wallets of the company's suits.

In the beginning the scheme worked. Curious about this "new" soft drink, consumers tried it and enjoyed it, and Crystal Pepsi generated more than $470 million in soft drink sales in its first year on the market. Unfortunately for PepsiCo, there wouldn't be a second year. Consumers apparently realized that they could get the same Pepsi taste from regular Pepsi (shocking!) and stopped buying the more expensive Crystal version. Crystal Pepsi was subsequently pulled from the shelves for good. Purity and cleanliness? Not in our soda!

THE SEE-THRU SODA TREND

After seeing how successful Crystal Pepsi was in its first year, Coca-Cola decided to copy Pepsi's lead and run with their version of a clear soft drink, Clear Tab, in December 1992. It too was pulled from the shelves after a little over a year.

1995

What Goes Up, Must Come Down

Throughout the trial prosecutors painted a chilling picture of a store owner more concerned with maximizing profits than customer safety, and of city officials willing to take bribes in exchange for allowing illegal design and construction.

—CNN.com

Following the Korean War, South Korea's commercialization boomed. Buildings went up and people flocked to the cities, but by building with speed, the Koreans sacrificed quality, and no building proved that more than the Sampoong Department Store.

The building, which was intended to be a four-story office building, was completed in 1989 (under the not-so-close watch of chairman Lee Joon) as a five-story department store. The flaws in this project were evident from the start. The structure was built on a landfill (a nice, firm surface . . . oh wait . . .), the structural beams were designed to support only four floors (bah, that fifth floor won't make a difference!), support columns were cut away to install escalators, and the concrete was mixed with saltwater, which deteriorated the rebars that strengthened the building. Not a problem. After all, the barely supported fifth floor only contained a swimming pool, a water tank, and eight restaurants, among other things.

Just five years after the building's completion, cracks started to appear, and on June 29, 1995, they were too abundant to ignore. Executives fled the scene while management closed just the fifth floor and shut the air conditioning off—which was smart, because shutting off the AC has saved countless structurally impaired buildings from collapsing. Right. . . . Within hours, those cracks became loud bangs, which led to sinking floors, and then the entire structure collapsed causing $216 million in damages and 501 deaths. Homeowners, we'd advise against calling in Lee Joon to help you with a home repair. He does not come highly recommended on Angie's List.

1998

THE ST. CLOUD GAS EXPLOSION

Governor Arne Carlson says he's issued a blank check to emergency personnel in St. Cloud who are searching the rubble after a gas explosion that killed four people. . . . The governor says he was stunned by the devastation around the blast site . . . and he praised rescue workers for their quick response.

—United Press International

You've heard the saying that timing is everything? Well on December 11, 1998, the work crew sent from Cable Constructors, Inc. (CCI) learned that the hard way.

The crew had been sent out to repair a utility pole in St. Cloud, Minnesota. Unfortunately, they made a mistake somewhere along the line, and the supports anchoring the pole to the ground ruptured a gas pipe. Okay. Accidents happen. I'm sure they called their supervisor as soon as they smelled gas, and everything worked out just fine. But if that happened, we wouldn't be talking about them here.

In actuality, the crew didn't report the accident to their supervisor until almost forty minutes had passed. The supervisor, realizing the danger of the situation, called everyone he could, and the fire department arrived on site fifteen minutes later. The gas ignited less than a half hour later, killing four people and causing roughly $400,000 in damages. If the team responsible for the leak in the first place had just remembered their natural gas protocol and called someone as soon as they smelled gas, the whole situation may have been avoided. CCI was held responsible for the disaster.

WHAT THE HELL IS THAT SMELL?

Natural gas is actually odorless. The rotten-egg smell you associate with gas is added in as an early alert system. Why they made it smell like something that makes you throw up in your mouth, we'll never know.

1998

THE YAOUNDÉ TRAIN EXPLOSION

The trains collided in mid-afternoon Saturday and before the explosion, hundreds of bystanders rushed to scoop up oil gushing from the ruptured tankers.

—*Today's News Herald,* February 15, 1998

Black gold. Texas tea. Worldwide, countries have been addicted to oil (thanks George W.) for decades, and the little country of Cameroon is no exception.

On Valentine's Day in 1998, a freight train carrying crude oil from Cameroon's oil fields collided with another train, jumped the track, and started spewing oil out into the streets. Now, you may be thinking that the collision that caused the Yaoundé Train Explosion left hundreds of people wishing they hadn't run out to the store for teddy bears and candy hearts. Normally you'd be right, but here things took a bit of a twist.

The trains derailed in a fairly poor part of the country, and people were just desperate for money. Oil was so valuable in Cameroon at the time that bystanders waded into the crude and started to collect it to sell. Too bad one gentleman in particular didn't think things through and continued to puff away on his cigarette while he was scooping up oil with his bare hands. Hey, some people smoke after sex, some smoke when they drink, and some smoke while illegally collecting petroleum. No judgment . . . okay, that's a lie. Let's take a few minutes and judge this guy. Oil! Lit cigarettes! Hello!

This guy dropped his cigarette into the ocean of oil that he was wading through and sparked an explosion that flattened the neighborhood, killed more than 120 people, and cut train service to the area for weeks. Nicely done, sir. Next time, try a nicotene patch.

1998

LOVE THAT DIRTY WATER

From July to September 1998, Bangladesh suffered the most extensive, deepest and longest lasting flooding of this century. An estimated one million homes were damaged, the main rice and other staple crops were lost due to flooding, and some 30 million persons in 6 million families were affected by the floods.

—Disasters Emergency Committee (DEC)

Every year for centuries, Bangladesh has flooded during the monsoon season between June and September. (Bet it's hard to get flood insurance . . .) Some of the flooding is normal and is needed to produce rice, one of the country's main crops. But lately, the floods have been doing more than just filling the rice fields.

In 1998, floodwaters covered more than 75 percent of the country between June and September. More than 1,000 people died and 30 million were left homeless, which doesn't make any sense. You'd think that with all that flooding year after year, people would have come up with some kind of a solution. Seriously, 80 percent of Bangladesh lies in a flood plain, and nearly the whole country sits only one meter above sea level. One word: Houseboats, people. Houseboats.

But Bangladesh isn't doing much to help itself out in other ways, either. Deforestation in the Himalayas is letting more water flow into the already swollen Ganges and Bramaputra Rivers that run through the country. Deforestation is also causing more silt to collect in the rivers, which decreases the rivers' depths and makes flooding almost unavoidable. So go ahead, Bangladesh. Cut down trees. Build more homes. Who cares about the environment anyway? But if you're not going to take Mother Nature into consideration, seriously, get a houseboat.

1998

WHO LOST THE DEATH POOL?

He was eating breakfast when he heard about it. He got a laugh out of it.
—Linda Hope, Bob Hope's daughter

Bob Hope had a great life: He had an illustrious career as a comedian, actor, and humanitarian; a couple of wives; and was given an honorary Academy Award. He played golf with Tiger Woods (before Woods was exposed as a womanizing scumbag), received the Ronald Reagan Freedom Award and the Congressional Gold Medal, and was made an honorary Knight Commander of the Order of the British Empire by Queen Elizabeth II. He was so well loved that you'd think everyone would want him to live forever, and he almost did. He died at the ripe old age of 100 in 2003, but his death was announced several times beforehand. Looks like some people were eager to cross him off their death list.

In 1998, the Associated Press mistakenly announced Hope's death on their website. News of his "passing" made it all the way to Congress where Dick Armey, the Speaker of the House of Representatives, ordered Representative Bob Stump to make the announcement of Hope's death. No one took the news well, and by the time they realized that it was all a big misunderstanding, the news had already spread around the world. Armey was forced to rescind his statement later on that day, but the damage had already been done. Guess you really can't trust a politician.

GOD SAVE THE BBC

The BBC Radio announced Queen Elizabeth II's death on May 17, 2010. The announcer was stopped and eventually admitted that he meant the whole thing as a joke. Bet clearing that one up was a royal pain in the ass.

1999

IT'S A BIRD . . . IT'S A DINOSAUR . . . IT'S AN ARCHAEORAPTOR!

How did we get into this mess?
—William Allen, *National Geographic* editor in chief

In 1999, paleontologists thought they found what they had been looking for: the evolutionary link between dinosaurs and birds. The animal was officially named *Archaeoraptor liaoningensis* and was unveiled at a *National Geographic* press conference and then later featured in the November 1999 issue of the magazine. Unfortunately, *National Geographic*, a highly esteemed magazine, didn't do their legwork, and the bones in the archaeoraptor were found to belong to as many as five different other dinosaurs.

Turns out that the fossils were from China where there was a healthy black market for dinosaur bones. To get a higher price, a Chinese farmer glued the various fossils together and sold it as a complete animal. *National Geographic* was in such a rush to get the news of the "new" dinosaur out there that they didn't bother to have any articles on the animal peer reviewed by other scientists who would have told them that the skeleton was a phony. In fact, the article *National Geographic* published in the November 1999 edition was actually written by their art editor, Christopher P. Sloan. What did an art editor know about dinosaurs? That's right. Not much. *National Geographic* admitted their mistake in their October 2000 edition. That's right, NatGeo: Open mouth. Insert foot.

1998

THE GREAT ZIPPERGATE

Now, I have to go back to work on my State of the Union speech. And I worked on it until pretty late last night. But I want to say one thing to the American people . . . I did not have sexual relations with that woman, Miss Lewinsky. I never told anybody to lie, not a single time; never. These allegations are false. And I need to go back to work for the American people. Thank you.

—President Bill Clinton

U.S. president Bill Clinton may not have been clear on what the term "sexual relations" really means, but in 1998 all of American learned that he'd been up to something fishy during his first year in the White House.

His affair with now-infamous White House intern Monica Lewinsky, which involved some "oral debate" and a fun game with a cigar tube, caused his impeachment, the suspension of his right to practice law, and a $90,000 charge for giving false testimony. You'd think that neither the married Clinton nor the twenty-one-year-old intern would have blabbed about their affair, but you'd be wrong. Apparently Lewinsky confided in her donkey-faced coworker Linda Tripp (who later had plastic surgery to remedy that particular problem), who decided to record all the telephone conversations the two women had to prove Lewinsky's involvement with her boss. What a great friend! Tripp also talked Lewinsky out of dry-cleaning a dress she had worn during one passionate encounter with the leader of the free world so she could use it to prove Clinton's wrongdoing.

Who knows what party is more to blame here: Lewinsky for being friends with someone as underhanded as Linda Tripp—or for being dirty enough to hang on to a dress with Clinton's foreign policy splashed all over it—or Clinton for having a little too much fun in the Oval Office. But any way you look at it, everyone involved was caught with their proverbial presidential briefs down.

1999

EXCITE'S EXCITING OPPORTUNITY . . . THROWN AWAY

They [Excite] don't have any defensible proprietary content that anybody really needs.

—Patrick Keane, online research analyst, 2001

New Excite CEO George Bell was looking to make a splash in the dot-com boom of the late 1990s. In 1997, he purchased an online shopping network, NetBot, for $35 million. A short time later, he purchased iMall (an e-commerce site) for around $425 million in stocks. Up next, in 1998, was Blue Mountain, an online e-card company, for $780 million. That's over $1.24 billion in a year's time if you're keeping track at home. However, it's the next $1 million he didn't spend that earned him a spot in this book.

Larry Page and Sergey Brin, the masterminds behind Google, were offering their newest creation to other companies, and Excite was interested. The initial offer? Just $1 million dollars. After spending $1.24 billion in a year, what's another million? Bell said no. Page and Brin offered to drop the price to $750,000—again, this is for Google—and an exasperated Bell insisted he wasn't interested. Did Bell turn into a tightwad overnight? What was the problem?

Page and Brin are still actively involved in Google's operations as the company generated around $6.5 billion in revenue in 2009. As for Excite? They filed for Chapter 11 two years after the failed deal. Sometimes, in the case of Google, the best deals are the ones you don't make!

> ## IF IT MAKES YOU FEEL BETTER . . .
> Excite shouldn't feel so bad. AltaVista and Yahoo! also passed on the Google offer. Yahoo! recovered nicely. AltaVista is another story.

1999

THE THRILL OF VICTORY AND THE
AGONY OF DEFEAT

*The ball was lying so good, I took my 2-iron. . . . I pushed it a little. I
didn't hit a very good shot.*

—Jean Van de Velde

Jean Van de Velde was one hole away from becoming the first Frenchman
in ninety-two years to win golf's historic British Open. Unfortunately, the
French would have to wait a little longer to celebrate.

Van de Velde approached the par-four eighteenth hole—a hole he birdied
in two prior rounds—with a three-shot lead. Bringing home the trophy
looked like a mere formality at this point, but Van de Velde proved that it was
anything but when his first shot landed in the rough just a few feet from the
water. Playing it safe would probably have been a good idea at this point, but
he motioned for the crowd to move so he could go for the green on his second
shot. Predictably, the ball careened off the grandstand, hit a rock, and found
high weeds. Zut alors! Then, on his third shot, Van de Velde's club got tangled
on his downswing and the ball ended up floating harmlessly into the muddy
water. Could it possibly get any worse? The answer is yes. Off come the shoes
as Van de Velde ponders shooting from the mud but decides against it. Taking
a drop (and a one-shot penalty), his next shot finds the bunker. He chips out
and putts in to complete a triple bogey, sending him into a three-way tie that
would be settled by a playoff, which he would lose. From hero to zero, all in
one hole.

I wonder if *Van de Velde* is French for "f*#k up"?

2000

Y2K: THE END OF THE WORLD?

The Y2K problem is the electronic equivalent of the El Niño and there will be nasty surprises around the globe.

—John Hamre, U.S. deputy secretary of defense

When computers were first introduced, the idea of shortening the year from 19xx to just xx in programming saved time, space, and energy for all of those involved. But with a new millennium approaching, it was widely assumed that global chaos would ensue once the year 2000 rolled around. What would those programs do? Would they spew error messages? Stop working altogether? Customers with HSBC bank received an early scare on December 28, 1999, when thousands of credit card swipe machines no longer worked and their transactions had to be processed on paper. Could this be the beginning of the end?

As the clock hit midnight on January 1, 2000, everyone stopped and held their collective breath . . . and nothing happened. That Y2K thing was really something, wasn't it?

Aside from a handful of slot machines in Delaware that stopped functioning and the wrong time being displayed on the master clock on the U.S. Naval Observatory's website, the whole thing was just a months-long media hype.

YOU GOTTA LOVE MODERN TECHNOLOGY

Larger problems actually surfaced in 2010 (or Y2K+10—how creative!). Due to a mix-up in the binary and decimal coding of digits, those computer programs couldn't recognize the "10." In Germany, over 20 million bank cards became unusable, and Windows Mobile messages had a sent date of 2016 instead of 2010. Where was the media for this one?

2001

ENRON'S CHARMED LIFE

The Enron scandal grew out of a steady accumulation of habits and values and actions that began years before and finally spiraled out of control.

—Bethany McLean and Peter Elkind, authors, *The Smartest Guys in the Room*

Enron. Mentioning the name has you laughing, but no one was laughing in their offices in 2001 when Enron became the biggest embarrassment of the financial world.

Enron set up their complicated financial reports to try and keep their numbers in the black by ensuring high income, high assets, and low liabilities, even if it meant being, well, inaccurate in its reporting. Once the Bad Reporting Snowball was pushed down the hill, it was nearly impossible to stop it.

Outside sources wondered how Enron's stock was so high, given that there was no way to know where its income was coming from. Enron execs started getting defensive when they were being peppered with questions about their "hidden" situation and how they weren't disclosing all of their financial information as all other companies did. Then, in August, Jeffrey Skilling stepped down as CEO just months after he sold at least 450,000 Enron shares. Insiders sensed the inevitable, and three months later, the inevitable happened. With shares down to sixty-one cents each, Enron filed for Chapter 11 protection.

Ignorance is bliss, but when the entire financial world is breathing down your neck, you can't run and you can't hide.

SHARING THE SPOTLIGHT

It didn't take long for the Next Big Thing in financial scandals to hit. July 2002 saw WorldCom file for Chapter 11 protection after fraudulent activity was discovered on their statements. The early 2000s were a bad time to try something tricky with the books.

2002

I COULD SWEAR THEY WERE HERE A SECOND AGO!

Simply stated, there is no doubt that Saddam Hussein now has weapons of mass destruction (WMDs).

—Dick Cheney, then vice president of the United States

When you come out in public and make a statement like that, with the job title of vice president, you'd better be damn sure you're right. Cue the losing horns from *The Price Is Right*.

Based on information that was revealed in the elder Bush's presidency a decade earlier, Hussein had indirectly indicated that WMDs were prevalent in Iraq during Operation Desert Storm. Different facilities were inspected throughout the 1990s in Iraq, culminating in 1998 with the belief that there were no WMDs present. An eight-year search with no results? Seems like a strong case, but Hussein kept pushing back at accusations that WMDs were around. Those were awfully strong words for a man presumably with nothing to hide. Then again, would you believe him? George W. Bush and his administration sure didn't, so they forced Iraq to disarm with the help of the UN Security Council under Resolution 1441.

No evidence was found that led to the development of WMDs, but Bush still wasn't buying it. Rather than wait for complete compliance with Resolution 1441, Bush invaded Iraq instead, hoping to play the role of hero and find them himself. Shockingly, there were none! The Iraq Survey Group concluded that the damage done during the Gulf War a decade earlier was enough to prevent Iraq from continuing its efforts with WMDs. Remember that one, Dubya, the war your dad helped start? Face it, they aren't there.

2002

KEEP THE COFFEE COMING

All trains are in good shape and at the highest degree of efficiency and
they are reviewed completely and regularly.
—Egyptian prime minister Atef Obeid

The month of February is a busy travel time in Egypt and on February 20,
2002, it seemed like everyone in the country wanted to get going at the same
time.

The train to Luxor departed from Cairo, Egypt, at double its capacity,
and it was only about forty miles into its journey when a fire broke out in the
cafeteria car. Supposedly, the fire was started by a portable gas fire that was
used to heat coffee. Why Egyptians were still using an open flame to heat their
coffee on a moving locomotive, the world will never know. The train continued
on its journey as the fire spread throughout roughly a half-dozen cars of the
overly crowded train. With no way for the train conductors to communicate
with the driver (it's 2002, people! Get a walkie-talkie or something!), the train
chugged on for hours before the driver knew what happened. By the time
the driver caught on, dozens of passengers had jumped out of the windows
and chaos had ensued as people rushed from one train car to the next. There
are no confirmed reports on the total number of people who were affected
by the fire. Why? Because, on top of everything else that went wrong, there
wasn't a ticket system in place—thus the train overcrowding. We don't know
why Egypt couldn't figure out the concept of a ticket or buy an electric coffee
pot, but the official death toll of the incident was 383, making it the deadliest
railway accident in Egypt's history. If you ever find yourself traveling to or in
Egypt, consider taking a bus.

2003

A Foul Play on a Foul Ball

Again in the air, down the left field line. Alou reaching into the stands and couldn't get it and is livid with a fan.

—Thom Brennaman, Fox Sports

Five outs. That's all the Cubs needed in 2003 to reach the World Series. The first potential out of those five is among the most infamous in baseball history.

With the Cubs ahead three games to two in the series and 3–0 in the eighth inning of Game 6, Luis Castillo hit a fly ball down the left-field line. Moises Alou gave chase to it toward the wall, and as he raised his glove, the ball bounced away into the stands as several fans reached for the free souvenir. Steve Bartman's hands were the first to touch it, and all eyes in Wrigley were on him—including those of a heated Moises Alou. A home fan preventing the home team from recording an out in a postseason game? Who gave him a ticket? In all, the Marlins would score eight runs in the inning, and the perpetrator of it all, Luis Castillo, came up again in the inning and recorded the third out. Bartman wasn't there to see it as he was escorted out of the park for his own safety. The Cubs would lose Game 7 and the series the next day.

If Moises Alou had caught that ball, Steve Bartman would be just another Cubs fan. Instead, he's public enemy number one among Cubs fans.

BLAME IT ON . . . THE GOAT?

A local tavern owner was removed from a Cubs World Series game in 1945 for the odor emanating from his pet goat. He later accosted the Cubs by saying, "You are never going to win a World Series again because you insulted my goat." Sixty-five years later, they haven't even been to the World Series. Who knew Nostradamus owned a tavern in Chicago?

2003

No Move Is a Bad Move

Pedro Martinez has been our man all year long and in situations like that, he's the one we want on the mound over anybody we can bring out of that bullpen.

—Grady Little, Red Sox manager, 2003

As a manager, the in-game decisions are yours to make. You have final say. Games and seasons can hinge on one decision, one call. Just ask Grady Little.

The Red Sox and Yankees were playing Game 7 in the 2003 ALCS. With Boston up 5–3 in the eighth inning, the Yankees had started to rally off of Red Sox starter Pedro Martinez and Sox fans started to grumble. With a runner at first base and one out, Grady ventured out to the mound. Here's what he had to work with:

- Opponents from all teams had a .208 batting average against Pedro in the first 100 pitches of his outing, and they hit .298 from the 101st pitch on.
- Pedro reached the 101-pitch mark in the eighth inning, and two of the best hitters in the Yankee's lineup were due up next.

Grady had relievers at the ready, but Pedro said he was fine (and what pitcher wouldn't say that under the circumstances?). Grady left Pedro in, which turned out to have dire consequences. A single and two doubles later, the game was tied 5–5. Then, finally, Grady pulled Pedro. But it was way too little, too late. Three innings later, the Yankees hit a walk-off home run that took them to the World Series and Grady Little was fired, which wasn't nearly enough of a punishment for Sox fans. Grady, next time just manage the game. All you have to do is your job!

2003

Grizzly Man's Last Voyage

He called me as he was leaving, and said, "I'll see you sometime in October if I don't die up there."

—David Wallace, writer, *Malibu Times*

You've heard of kids being raised by wolves? Well, Tim Treadwell, a.k.a. Grizzly Man, tried to integrate himself into a pack of grizzly bears by spending thirteen summers living amongst them. The thirteenth summer would certainly turn out to be an unlucky one.

In 2002, Treadwell dragged his unwilling girlfriend, Amie Huguenard, up to Katmai National Park in Alaska to introduce her to his new "family." Huguenard was petrified of bears—and, really, who isn't?—but unwisely decided to humor her boyfriend. To make matters worse, Treadwell pretty much threw safety to the wind when they were up there: He made camp right next to a salmon stream (a popular bear buffet) at a time of year when food was in short supply. He also refused to set up an electric fence and to carry pepper spray, both offenses that he had been cited for in the past. Not surprisingly, both Treadwell and Huguenard ended their camping trip inside the bears. On October 6, what was left of Tim and Amie was found at their campsite by the air pilot who had arrived to pick them up. Maybe one of the bears asked the unlucky couple who'd been sleeping in her bed . . . and didn't like the answer.

IN REMEMBRANCE

Tim Treadwell's journey can be relived for all to see in the 2005 documentary film *Grizzly Man*. Too bad the DVD doesn't come with an alternate ending.

2003

DON'T HOLD YOUR BREATH!

Hong Kong's streets are eerily empty. The jostling, noisy crowds that characterize this fast-paced city have retreated in fear. For a city that depends on the service sector to generate 86% of its gross domestic product and is powered with hundreds of thousands of small businesses, this disease could be a real economic killer.

—Mark L. Clifford, *BusinessWeek*

An ad slogan, when prepared properly, can bring forth spectacular results. And in 2003, the Hong Kong Tourism Board came up with a new slogan to help promote tourist activities in their country: Hong Kong: It'll Take Your Breath Away. Makes sense. Hong Kong is a country known for its sprawling skyline and natural harbor. It is bound to have aspects that would leave any tourist breathless.

Unfortunately, it was a slow news day in the boardroom when they thought up this slogan. Right outside their office and all throughout Hong Kong, the deadly SARS epidemic was tearing through the nation. One of the main symptoms of SARS? Shortness of breath. The board didn't catch their play on words until it was too late. The ad had made its way into the British versions of popular magazines such as *Cosmopolitan* and *Conde Nast Traveller* and was even being featured on Hong Kong billboards. Technically, there was truth to the slogan. Going to Hong Kong in 2003 could, literally, take your breath away. Just be sure to enter at your own risk—and wear a mask.

THE DEAN SCREAM

Not only are we going to New Hampshire, Tom Harkin, we're going to South Carolina and Oklahoma and Arizona and North Dakota and New Mexico, and we're going to California and Texas and New York . . . And we're going to South Dakota and Oregon and Washington and Michigan, and then we're going to Washington, D.C., to take back the White House! *Yeah!!!*

—Howard Dean, almost presidential nominee

Former Vermont governor Howard Dean started out his race to earn the Democratic presidential nomination in good form. He was a great fundraiser. He opposed George W. Bush's invasion of Iraq. And he had a really good chance of winning the Democratic presidential nomination. And then he opened his mouth after he finished third in the Iowa caucus and out it came: "the Dean Scream." The nail in his candidacy's coffin.

Dean was trying to get his supporters pumped up about his campaign and started to yell the names of states he planned to win. He said that he was shouting to be heard over the crowd, and the microphone he was wearing only picked up his voice, which made the whole thing seem even more insane than it was. But even Dean called his "I have a scream" speech a "crazy, red-faced rant."

Dean's campaign was finished. His approval ratings plummeted, and he withdrew from the race less than a month later. Guess screaming isn't presidential. Who knew?

2004

DOWN IN FRONT, LARRY!

In God We Trust - Vengeance is mine sayeth the Lord - No Fear.
—Tattoo on Larry Desmedt's neck

Larry Desmedt became famous as a stuntman and a motorcycle builder. Turns out he didn't have much use for the seat on his bikes.

Larry was performing his signature stunt at a rally in Concord, North Carolina, in August 2004, where he would stand on the motorcycle while it was moving. Larry had his protective suit on, but for some reason he passed on wearing the helmet. Its one thing to be brash, but it's a whole different ballgame if you're going to be stupid. Even though he considered it one of his easier stunts, it didn't go off without a hitch. The motorcycle wobbled underneath him, causing Larry to lose his balance and hit his head on the way down. He died two days later from his injuries. Ironically enough, North Carolina has a mandatory helmet law for motorcycle riders of all ages. Someone forgot to fill Larry in on the concept that the law applies while standing as well as sitting!

FOR THOSE WHO DO SIT

There are still three states—Illinois, Iowa, and New Hampshire—that have no laws requiring the use of a helmet when riding a motorcycle. Be careful for those that may be standing on bikes, too!

2004

NIPPLEGATE

I am sorry if anyone was offended by the wardrobe malfunction during the halftime of the Super Bowl. It was not intentional and is regrettable.

—Justin Timberlake

Ah, Super Bowl XXXVII. Memorable for so many reasons. The New England Patriots defeated the Carolina Panthers 32–29. And Tom Brady was named MVP for the second time in three years. *Sports Illustrated* writer Peter King even called it "the greatest Super Bowl of all time." But he probably only said that because all of America got an eyeful of Janet Jackson's nipple.

Jackson and Justin Timberlake were performing Timberlake's hit, "Rock Your Body," when he reached over, pulled off part of Jackson's outfit, and exposed her right breast to all 144.4 million viewers. Within minutes, complaints started flowing in—and those who weren't complaining were busy rewinding their TiVo.

The effects of Jackson's boobilicious moment were felt far and wide. The FCC went crazy fining everyone they could think of and setting up tape delays for every other event that happened that year. The Victoria's Secret Fashion Show was canceled because the producers were afraid that women in underwear were just too much for the American public. And, amidst a swirl of controversy that claimed Jackson's coming-out party was planned, Janet and Justin abashedly apologized to the public.

I don't know what's more of a disaster here: the fact that millions of Americans think that seeing a nipple on TV is the worst thing that could ever happen or that Justin and Janet ruined TV for years afterward with their cockamamie scheme. I mean, really, what kind of boobs would even think of something like that?

2005

SIX OF ONE, A HALF DOZEN OF THE OTHER

It's absurd that the exchange doesn't have any system to reject such incomprehensible orders.

—Takao Saga, senior economist at the Japan Securities Research Institute

It's a common saying in the carpentry world that you measure twice, cut once to avoid critical mistakes. Maybe a similar saying should be invoked in the world of stockbrokers.

Mizuho Securities, an investment banking and securities firm based in Japan, had issued an order to sell one share of stock in J-COM Ltd. (a staffing company) for 610,000 yen (approx. $5,042). Instead, the order was placed as selling 610,000 shares for one yen a piece. What a bargain! Immediately realizing the error, Mizuho put forth several orders to cancel the transaction. Unfortunately, due to a glitch in the Tokyo Stock Exchange's (TSE) computers, even though the cancellation orders were received, they weren't processed and the bargain-basement stock sale was put through. Total losses: 40.7 million yen (about $375,000). Now that's an expensive f*#k up!

But the drama wasn't over yet, and Mizuho filed suit against the TSE to recoup the losses incurred by the unreported errors. It took four years for the court to render its decision, and the TSE was deemed liable due to their negligent system but was only considered to be 70 percent at fault. Mizuho is appealing this decision and it is ongoing in the court system.

Maybe the folks at Mizuho should reconsider their stock-selling methods—and double-check the math abilities of their stockbrokers—if they want to avoid selling shares of stocks worth $5,000 for a little over a penny a piece!

2006

WHAT'S A LITTLE BIRDSHOT BETWEEN FRIENDS

[Harry] Whittington downed a bird and went to retrieve it. While he was out of the hunting line, another covey was flushed and Cheney swung on a bird and fired, striking Whittington in the face, neck and chest.

—The Texas Parks and Wildlife Department

So apparently seventy-eight-year-old attorney Harry Whittington looks a lot like a quail, or at least that's what then Vice President Dick Cheney thought when he shot his friend full of birdshot on February 11, 2006.

The two men were letting off some steam as part of a hunting party on a ranch in Texas. Whittington bent over to pick up a bird he had hit and Cheney opened fire. Next thing Whittington knew, he was lying on the ground next to his prey. (Poetic justice perhaps?) Aside from the more than 200 pieces of birdshot littering his body, Whittington also suffered a heart attack and a collapsed lung as a result of the shooting. Cheney chalked the whole thing up as an accident and not-so-happily watched his and President Bush's approval ratings continue to tank.

What did Whittington have to say about the whole thing? According to MSNBC, all he said was, "My family and I are deeply sorry for all that Vice President Cheney has had to go through this past week. We hope that he will continue to come to Texas and seek the relaxation that he deserves." What a guy. Cheney shoots him and gives him a heart attack and Whittington just wishes that everyone would stop beating up on Mr. VP. Whittington is either the nicest person in the world, or he knows that Cheney won't hesitate to pull the trigger. Either way, it's always best to keep your friends close and your enemies closer, especially if they're carrying a gun.

2006

A MILLION LITTLE MISTAKES

James Frey is here and I have to say it is difficult for me to talk to you because I feel really duped. But more importantly, I feel that you betrayed millions of readers. I think it's such a gift to have millions of people to read your work and that bothers me greatly.

—Oprah

Any author who manages to get his book selected for Oprah's book club is a pretty lucky guy. After all, all Oprah has to do is think about liking something and millions of people are grabbing that book/toy/electronic device off the shelves faster than little sweatshop kids in India can pump them out. In October 2005, James Frey became the lucky recipient of Oprah's favor when she read his "memoir" *A Million Little Pieces*; due to Oprah's endorsement the book sold more than 3.5 million copies and spent more than fifteen weeks on the *New York Times* bestseller list. Oprah even defended Frey when Larry King asked him about a report published on thesmoking-gun.com that said the events in the book weren't true. But Oprah's love affair with Frey didn't last long.

On January 26, 2006, Oprah invited Frey back onto her show and basically ripped him a new one. She said that she felt "duped and disappointed," but things got even better when Oprah brought out Frey's publisher, Nan Talese from Random House, to explain why Talese marketed the book as a memoir without bothering to fact-check Frey's stories. She didn't have an answer, and Oprah continued her massacre.

So let this be a lesson to all you prospective authors out there. If Oprah endorses your book, don't lie to her—or she'll rip you into a million little pieces on live TV.

2007

WHEN YOU GOTTA GO, YOU GOTTA GO

We were stunned when we heard the news. We are awaiting information
that will help explain how this tragic event occurred.

—John Geary, Entercom Sacramento VP and marketing manager

In 2007, KDND-FM (a.k.a. The End) in Sacramento held a radio contest, "Hold Your Wee for a Wii," to promote the wildly popular Nintendo Wii system. Contestants were to drink water and hold their wee as long as possible without using a restroom. Sounds benign, right? Not so much.

As soon as the radio broadcast of the content started up, the warnings started to trickle in. A nurse informed the medically challenged crew at the station that water intoxication could kill the contestants. Their response? They said they were "aware of it." Interesting. More callers reminded the DJs on the show about a college student in nearby Chico, California, who died just two years earlier from water intoxication. Again, nothing. As the saying goes, those who don't learn from history are doomed to repeat it. And, not shockingly, history was repeated. The contestant who came in second place, Jennifer Lea Strange, complained of an intense headache after the contest and was found dead of water intoxication just an hour later. Way to listen to medical advice, KDND! As a result, ten station employees connected to the show were let go, and in 2009 the station was no longer operating.

WHO KNEW?

It's recommended that humans consume one to two liters of water per day depending on body mass. Drink significantly more and water can be considered dangerous to your health!

2007

TRUSS NO ONE

Although the Board's investigation is still on-going and no determination of probable cause has been reached, interim findings in the investigation have revealed a safety issue that warrants attention . . .

—Mark V. Rosenker, National Transportation Safety Board chairman

The I-35W Mississippi River bridge was crossed by roughly 140,000 vehicles a day and was Minnesota's fifth-busiest bridge. But it looks like the bridge needed a little downtime because during rush hour on August 1, 2007, the bridge collapsed into the Mississippi River, killing thirteen people and sending an additional 145 to the emergency room. Now, bridges don't just fall down without any warning—and in fact, various inspectors had given a number of heads ups over the years, including the following:

- 1990: The bridge was deemed "structurally deficient."
- 2006: You guessed it! Still structurally deficient and Minnesota governor Tim Pawlenty finally agreed that some parts of the bridge need to be reinforced sooner than later.
- 2007: The bridge reinforcement was cancelled because bridge officials were worried that any work would weaken the bridge and cause it to fail. Hmm . . .

When the bridge collapsed in August 2007, some work had just been completed, many of the lanes were closed for repaving, and there were thousands of pounds of construction equipment sitting around. Looks like whoever made those decisions didn't get the memo about how dangerous the bridge was. You know, the memos that had been coming in for the past *seventeen years*! You know how anything government related moves slowly, but this was ridiculous!

2008

From Moment of Truth to Moment of Fiction

Perhaps some of it was then, "If I'm going to end my marriage, then if I can win a hundred thousand or two hundred thousand dollars. I can start a new life with some cash in my pocket."

—Howard Schultz, executive producer, *Moment of Truth*

Lauren Cleri was a contestant on the short-lived Fox game show *Moment of Truth*, a game show where contestants took a lie detector test and then had to truthfully answer those same questions on the air to win some cash. The catch was that if a contestant lied about any answer, he'd/she'd lose all the money earned and pretty much be laughed off the show.

Cleri tested the limits of her family's unconditional love by admitting to stealing from a prior employer, fantasizing about an ex-boyfriend on the altar, cheating on her husband, and then stating that she wished she had married that ex-boyfriend instead of her husband . . . who was sitting right there! Her honesty had already earned her $100,000, and the next question would bring her winnings to $200,000. The question? "Do you think you're a good person?" With Cleri's dirty laundry littering the stage, the money was practically hers . . . except that she answered yes and it registered as a lie. And what a lie it was. Gone was all of the money she had won. Gone was her marriage (her husband filed for divorce two months after the show). And gone was any potential job opportunity she may have been looking for from the show. Someone should have told Cleri that the truth would set her free, but a lie would only serve to make her a game-show laughingstock.

2009

EGYPTIAN TRAIN CRASH

Reuters Television images showed two crumpled carriages. It also showed the corpse of a cow under the wheels of one of the trains. [The Middle East News Agency], citing witnesses, said the first train had stopped after it struck the cow.

—Reuters.com

Egypt has a pretty bad history when it comes to trains (see Keep the Coffee Coming, 2002), and in October 2009, their safety record pretty much went off the track. The culprits? A water buffalo and a train signalman who wanted to get home early.

The first train in the saga was running on schedule when the conductor saw a water buffalo on the tracks. Being an animal lover, he stopped to let the buffalo finish up whatever it was that it was doing before he got the train moving again. You gotta love this guy. He loves animals. And he put the word out that he was staying put until the cow went home.

Unfortunately, not everyone involved was quite so courteous. Sayyed Ali Tehewi, the signalman who was in charge of letting other trains know about the water buffalo delay, threw in the towel and left work early. However, his chances of playing hooky without his boss finding out went up in a fiery explosion of twisted metal when a second train slammed right into back of the train that was stopped on the track. (Apparently the second driver didn't see the "I brake for animals" sticker prominently placed on the train in front of him.) When all was said and done, eighteen people (including Tehewi) and one water buffalo were dead.

The irony? Tehewi actually left work early so he could catch a train home— the very same train that was involved in the accident.

GOOD STUFF! CHEAP!

We made it to Kansas City in one piece. We're visiting @noellhyman's family. Can't wait to get some good video while we're here. :-)

—Israel Hyman, via Twitter

The explosion of popularity in social networking websites in the late 2000s created a vast spectrum for anyone and everyone to post anything and everything about themselves. Information is out there that can be dangerous when put in the hands of the wrong people—especially those we accept as "friends" even though we've never met these people before.

Israel Hyman found this out the hard way in May 2009. A Twitter user, he posted a comment about how he was on vacation out of state and was hoping to have a good time. Some 2,000 followers saw this, and at least one decided to take advantage of it. Hyman returned from his vacation to find his home broken into. Thousands of dollars worth of electronics equipment were gone.

Who publicizes to a large group of people—not just close friends, but strangers as well—that you're not going to be home for a lengthy period of time? Why not just put a big sign on your front lawn saying "This House Is Empty—Take What You Want"? That's basically what you're doing when you post that kind of info on Twitter, Facebook, or wherever you do your "networking" so your "friends" can see it.

WHO'S CREEPIN' ON YOU?

The Co-Operative Insurance group revealed that 36 percent of social network website users in Britain give detailed accounts of their actions and whereabouts online, and 20 percent of all profiles are available for everyone—not just "friends"—to see. Think before you post.

2009

THE RED-HANDED BALLOON

You guys said that, um, we did this for the show.
—Falcon Heene, a.k.a. Balloon Boy

It's a bird! It's a plane! It's . . . Balloon Boy!

On October 15, 2009, the world was transfixed by the Heene family of Fort Collins, Colorado. They had been building a weird UFO-looking helium balloon for some time, but now the family was telling the authorities that the balloon had drifted off—with six-year-old Falcon Heene inside. If the first question that popped into your head was "Why were they building a humongous helium balloon in their backyard?", you were in the majority.

The balloon stayed afloat for roughly two hours. During this time it was reported that something had fallen off or out of the balloon, so volunteers and officials searched by foot for Falcon. Maybe they should have been searching for Falcon's parents' true motives.

Richard and Mayumi were fame whores who would do whatever it took to extend their fifteen minutes. One of Richard's associates even told the media that Richard was "a shameless self-promoter who would do almost anything to promote his latest endeavor." Take the "almost" out of there, and you have the truth. Falcon was found hiding in the garage and later told Larry King that his parents told him to hide there "for the show." I don't know if the Heene's first mistake was trusting a six year old to keep his mouth shut, but they clearly didn't think this thing through. Criminal charges were pressed, and both Richard and Mayumi were sentenced to jail time and community service. Hope it was worth it.

2010

F*#K Up at the Redneck Riviera

A team of researchers in the Gulf of Mexico say they found an oily layer as thick as two inches coating the sea floor in some places, and they believe it may be from the BP spill.

—CNN.com

On April 20, 2010, the Deepwater Horizon oil rig leased by oil giant BP exploded, killing eleven men and pouring 185 million gallons of oil into the Gulf of Mexico over the course of the next four months. BP's first mistake? Drilling 5,000 feet under the surface of the ocean without a plan in place on how to stop an oil leak. Can you imagine how that conversation went?:

BP Lackey: Hey, CEO, what do you think about deep-sea drilling without a backup plan in case something goes wrong?

BP CEO: Great idea! It'll all be fine. If the damn thing leaks, we'll just improvise!

Looks like improvising didn't work, however. By the time all was said and done, BP was taking ideas from everyone from the Army Corps of Engineers to Kevin Costner on how to stop the spill.

BP strongly disagrees, but the oil company took some shortcuts to save money and rush the drilling process that actually caused the disaster. For example, BP replaced the drill fluid that was supposed to keep the gas building up in the pipe away from the rig with saltwater, which wasn't heavy enough to keep the gas from its ignition source, and the blowout preventer, the oil well's kill switch, was connected to a temporary pipe instead of the one actually attached to the well.

By the time the much-watched oil well was sealed on September 19, 2010, irreversible damage was done to the Redneck Riviera's tourism industry and to the marine habitat in the Gulf. Hey, BP! Next time, have a backup plan. You cheap bastards!

2010

Someone Give the Owner an Owner's Manual

Heselden had suffered multiple blunt force injuries of the chest and spine consistent with a fall whilst riding a gyrobike.

—David Hinchcliff, coroner

The Segway PT (personal transporter) was the brainchild of Dean Kamen. The vehicle is propelled by the user leaning in the direction he/she intends to go. Unfortunately for Kamen, he didn't see much worldwide success with his device as several countries restricted its use in a variety of ways. No sidewalks, no going too fast, no operating it from 12:00 to 12:15 while talking on a cell phone and eating a sandwich . . . you name it and a country thought of a way to keep the Segway off the streets. However, a British investor, Jimi Heselden, thought of it as a solid investment opportunity and purchased the company in December 2009.

Nine months later, Heselden didn't exactly demonstrate a ringing endorsement for his own product. While riding the Segway along a footpath, he apparently leaned too much in one direction, plummeting eighty feet over the cliff and was dead upon the arrival of paramedics. Talk about an epic fail! The owner of the company dies less than a year after buying the very company whose product he was using? That would be like a marathon runner and fitness author dying while running (remember Jim Fixx, 1984?). C'mon, Jimi. Test-drive it before you buy it!

SO WHERE CAN I USE THIS?

Sixteen different countries have some sort of restrictions while using the Segway. Among the strictest is the United Kingdom, where it can only be used on private property with the owner's permission. Maybe the UK will institute "no riding near a cliff" next.

2010

THE IMPERFECT GAME

I didn't want this to be my 15 minutes of fame. I would have liked my 15 minutes to be a great call in the World Series. Hopefully, my 15 minutes are over now.

—Jim Joyce, MLB umpire

Those who came to Comerica Park in Detroit on June 2, 2010, for the Tigers/Indians game didn't know they were going to see a historical performance. They also didn't know that one man was going to take it away faster than you can say "f*#k up."

Tigers starter Armando Galarraga was coasting through the Indians lineup and was just one out away from the twentieth perfect game in MLB history. All that stood in his way was Indians shortstop Jason Donald—and first-base umpire Jim Joyce.

Donald hit a feeble ground ball between first and second. The Tigers first basemen, Miguel Cabrera, fielded the ball then flipped to Galarraga at first base. Galarraga stepped on the bag before Donald did for the twenty-seventh and final out. Or—as Jim Joyce saw it—the first hit.

Oh, Jim. Really? Replays showed that Galarraga beat Donald to the base by a whole half a step! When the ruling was made, Galarraga only mustered a smirk and kept quiet, but all 17,738 fans in attendance made sure to let Joyce know how they felt. Hey, Jim, if you didn't want that to be your fifteen minutes of fame, you should have made the right call.

YEAH, I F*#KED UP

Joyce did the honorable thing and fessed up to his f*#k up after the game. He tearfully apologized to Galarraga, and the pair shook hands at a pregame ceremony where Galarraga was presented with a Corvette from General Motors.

2010

———✦———

THE TRAIN TO NOWHERE

During the investigation, witnesses told deputies they were at the site in hopes of seeing a "ghost train."
—The Iredell County sheriff's office

On August 27, 1891, in Iredell County, North Carolina, a train jumped the tracks and plunged sixty-five feet into the flooded river below. Roughly thirty people died in the incident that is now know as the Bostian Bridge Train Tragedy.

What does this have to do with something that happened in 2010? Well, every year, groups of ghost hunters gather at the bridge to watch for the "ghost train" to come through. Supposedly, viewers were able to see the train, hear the crash, or see a ghost holding a gold watch. And where were they supposed to stand to see and hear this stuff? Oh, right. In the middle of a railroad bridge. Apparently no one ever thought that was an issue until it was too late.

Instead of seeing the ghost train, the group got a nasty surprise when an actual steel train came around the corner. An actual train on a railroad bridge? Who would have thunk it? The majority of the ghost hunters ran the 150 feet to safety, but one died in the accident.

So if you ever feel the crazy desire to stand in the middle of a railroad trestle, remember safety first, ghost hunting second.

═══ THE HAUNTING ═══

One of the top ten haunted places in the United States is the Whaley House in San Diego. The house was built over part of a cemetery in 1857, and numerous ghosts have been documented there. Sounds like a scene from *Poltergeist*, right? Check out the house at *www .whaleyhouse.org*.

INDEX

ABOUT THE AUTHORS

Ken Lytle earned his BA in communications with a concentration in journalism from Boston College. By day a mild-mannered accountant and by night a passionate trivia jockey who hosts bar trivia at hot spots all over the South Shore, Ken is the Superman of the bar trivia scene. An intensely loyal Boston sports fan, he is well accustomed to all-around sports disasters and stupid mistakes made by the teams he loves. He combined his love for words and numbers with his vast array of odd facts and figures to assemble this collection of catastrophes. He lives in Whitman, Massachusetts.

Katie Corcoran Lytle, MA, has long loved any and all trivial pursuits and put her love of arcane knowledge to use by earning her master's degree in nineteenth-century American literature. A former professor—and relative of *Titanic* victim Frank Millet—Katie currently works as a publishing professional. The useless knowledge she has acquired over the years doesn't help her out much in her everyday life, but it does make her great at dinner conversation and bar trivia, which she plays frequently. She lives in Whitman, Massachusetts.

Bob Carney is the founder and owner of nationwide bar trivia machine Stump! Trivia. He founded the company in 1999 and has expanded his trivia empire from four bars in Boston, Massachusetts, to hundreds of bars in states from New Hampshire to Hawaii. Bob lives in West Roxbury, Massachusetts. Check him out at *www.stumptrivia.com*.

DAILY BENDER

Want Some More?

Hit up our humor blog, The Daily Bender, to get your fill of all things funny—be it subversive, odd, offbeat, or just plain mean. The Bender editors are there to get you through the day and on your way to happy hour. Whether we're linking to the latest video that made us laugh or calling out (or bullshit on) whatever's happening, we've got what you need for a good laugh.

If you like our book, you'll love our blog. (And if you hated it, "man up" and tell us why.) Visit The Daily Bender for a shot of humor that'll serve you until the bartender can.

Sign up for our newsletter at

www.adamsmedia.com/blog/humor

and download our Top Ten Maxims No Man Should Live Without.